Did You See That?

Joe Sledge

Books by Joe Sledge

Did You See That? A GPS Guide to North Carolina's Out of the Ordinary Attractions
Did You See That? On The Outer Banks
Did You See That? Too!
Did You See That Ghost?
Haunting The Outer Banks
Nag's Head: Or, Two Months Among The Breakers (editor, annotations)

Fiction
Bess Truly And Her Zap-Gun Rangers

Did You See That?
A GPS guide to North Carolina's out of the ordinary attractions

Joe Sledge

© 2012, 2021 by Joe Sledge
Did You See That? Second Edition

All Rights Reserved

No part of this document may be reproduced or transmitted in any form or by any means, electronic, mechanical, photocopying, recording, or otherwise, without prior written permission of the author.

Photography and illustration credits are found at the end of this book and constitute an extension of this copyright page.
ISBN 978-0-9980968-7-2
Cover design by Daniel Ray Norris and Barb Noel.

This book is meant for entertainment in the form of describing North Carolina folklore and locations. Some of the stories are based in legend and cannot be verified and the author cannot guarantee their accuracy. Some of these places are on private property or in locations that would be dangerous to access. Do not go unless you have received permission by the correct people, are sure of the legality of entrance, and are sure of your personal safety, or you may face prosecution for trespassing or other crimes, as well as placing yourself in physical danger.

For all you roadrunners out there

Table Of Contents

Introduction *1*
Oddity *3*
Difficulty *4*
Going, Going... GONE! *5*

Coastal *7*
Manmade Palm Tree Wrightsville Beach *9*
Fort Fisher Hermit Fort Fisher *13*
Money Island Wilmington *19*
Price's Creek Lighthouse Southport *23*
Mary's Gone Wild Bottle Village Supply *25*
Operation Bumblebee Spotting Towers Topsail Beach *29*
Giant Alligator Surf City *31*
Original Wright Brothers Monument Kitty Hawk *33*
Wright Brothers Monument Plaque Kill Devil Hills *37*
Statue of Virginia Dare Manteo *41*
Silver UFO House Frisco *45*
British Cemetery Ocracoke *47*
Live Oaks Ocracoke *51*
World's Largest Hammock Point Harbor *53*
Giant Blimp Hangar Weeksville *55*
Floating Church Swan Quarter *59*
Belhaven Museum Belhaven *61*
Dugout Canoe Shipwrecks Lake Phelps *65*
Ram Albemarle Plymouth *69*

CSS Neuse & CSS Neuse II Kinston *73*
Self Kicking Machines New Bern *79*
Mysterious Hoofprints Bath *83*
Maco Light Maco *87*
World's Largest Frying Pan Rose Hill *91*
Brady C. Jefcoat Museum of Americana Murfreesboro *93*
Pactolus Light Pactolus & Stokes *95*

Central *99*
Pioneer Giant Shriner Roanoke Rapids *113*
Second Hardee's Rocky Mount *115*
Concrete Dinosaur Wilson *119*
Vollis Simpson's Whirligigs Wilson *121*
Tee the Tastee-Freez Twin Kenly *125*
Country Doctor Museum Bailey *127*
ShadowHawk Western Town Smithfield *129*
Hills of Snow Snowball Stand Smithfield *133*
Vander Light Between Vander and Steadman *137*
Arsenal "Ghost" Tower Fayetteville *141*
Eiffel Tower Fayetteville *143*
Former Grave of Robert E. Lee's Daughter Near Warrenton *145*
Soul City Soul City *147*
Giant Concrete Legs South Henderson *149*
Gotno Farm Raleigh *151*
Giant Ice Cream Bowl and Spoon Raleigh *155*
Giant Piano Between Durham and Raleigh *157*

Brontosaurus Durham ········· *159*
Robot Tobacco Farmer Durham ········· *161*
Giant Sundial Chapel Hill ········· *163*
Dunce Cap on Wilson Library Chapel Hill ········· *165*
Gimghoul Castle Chapel Hill ········· *167*
Clyde Jones Chainsaw Art Bynum ········· *171*
Occoneechee Raceway Hillsborough ········· *175*
Large Rocking Chair and Adirondack Hillsborough ········· *177*
Painted Barns Cameron ········· *179*
Shangri-La Prospect Hill ········· *183*
Aunt Bee's House Siler City ········· *185*
Devil's Tramping Ground Harper's Crossroads ········· *187*
First Miniature Golf Course in the US Pinehurst ········· *189*
World's Largest Strawberry Ellerbe ········· *191*
Mystery On-Ramp Mayodan ········· *193*
World's Largest Chest of Drawers High Point ········· *195*
Lydia's Ghost Jamestown ········· *199*
Big Red Bicycle High Point ········· *203*
Duncan Phyfe Chair Thomasville ········· *205*
Körner's Folly Kernersville ········· *207*
Shell Gas Station Winston Salem ········· *211*
Big Coffee Pot Winston-Salem ········· *213*
Fisk Tire Boy Rural Hall ········· *217*
Metalmorphosis Charlotte ········· *219*
Love Valley Western Town Love Valley ········· *221*

Mountains *225*
Tom Dula's Grave Ferguson *225*
Mystery Hill Blowing Rock *229*
Land of Oz Beech Mountain *233*
Brown Mountain Lights near Morganton *237*
Quilt Block Vertical Sundial Burnsville *241*
Andrews Geyser Old Fort *243*
The Urban Trail Asheville *245*
Lake Lure Church Bell Lake Lure *247*
Morris the Tryon Horse Tryon *251*
Harry's Grille and Piggy's Ice Hendersonville *253*
Look Homeward Angel Statue Hendersonville *255*
PARI Radio Telescopes Rosman *257*
Bear Shadow Cashiers *261*
Judaculla Rock Cullowhee *263*
The Fugitive Train Wreckage Dillsboro *265*
Santa's Land Theme Park Cherokee *269*
The Chiefs of Cherokee Cherokee *271*
Road to Nowhere Bryson City *275*
World's Largest Ten Commandments Murphy *277*

Afterword *281*
Acknowledgements *282*
About The Author *285*

Introduction

"North Carolina has been the home for unique oddities for decades, even hundreds of years"

When I first wrote those words, I thought I was writing for people like me, who liked to discover something strange or odd hidden behind a tangle of kudzu or half buried in sand. To be honest, I was wrong about them. And wrong about me. The trip became as important as the discovery. The people who bought the first edition of this book weren't really looking for a destination, but a journey.

North Carolina, from Manteo to Murphy, is about 550 miles long, and it's chock full of places to explore that many of us have never seen, much less heard of. There's a story behind every old building, every general store, every statue in a little village. And that's why I wrote this book.

Growing up on the coast, I knew my way around that part of the state. But going inland, especially to the mountains, it meant speeding by the little towns, the enticing signs, those great stop offs that every kid's parents either dread or don't have time for. I couldn't stop at those places when I was young. We had places to be. Now, we have places to go.

Yes, I love the hidden bits of history and the strange art that has been created by my fellow North Carolina residents. Curiosity and discovery have driven the writing of this book. But what I really like, now, almost twelve years later, is not so much the things I found and wrote about, but the cities and towns I pass through. I can see a sign for a town and just know that there's something interesting down there, or there used to be long ago. That's what has become the best thing about writing and reading this book, as well as meeting so many people who like these journeys as much as I do.

Map technology has changed so much since I first wrote this book. Just about every new car has a screen in it now, and everyone has a map in their pocket now that can take them to these locations. This book still helps by giving the location in latitude and longitude, which makes it a little easier to find all the places I have listed, but it's a lot easier now. So with that, I think my original charge from the first edition still has meaning.

It is my hope that this book helps to preserve the stories and places so unique to North Carolina. But I must challenge the reader. Don't just read this book. Use it to get out and find every place you can. Hopefully, you will find things that even I didn't know existed. Just keep looking, people. Start here, finish out there somewhere.

Oddity

A one to five star rating of just how strange the attraction is. Is it something you can see somewhere else? Or nowhere else? Does it fit in or stick out like a sore thumb? Just how odd, how unbelievable, does this thing get? Well, this will help tell you.

★ It makes sense that this is here. I just didn't know about it. These are fitting for the locale, but may be hidden or unknown parts of history.

★★ You don't see that every day, unless you live here. Something different, but it still seems like part of the community. It may be less odd than one would think.

★★★ Whoa, how did they do that? It doesn't fit in, or it has a unique history about it. But, when you learn more about it, it's a little less weird.

★★★★ I hope it doesn't come to life! These are the truly strange stories, places and legends that are hard to believe. It only gets stranger when you discover that the weird stories told about them are all true.

★★★★★ I've never seen that before! Now, let's get outta here! These make the visitor truly uncomfortable. Scary, odd, or incredibly different, this doesn't belong, and you are probably not the only one who feels this way.

Difficulty

How hard is it to find this thing? How about getting to it? Can you touch it? Do you even want to? See this rating to tell you how easy it is to find.

★ You can see it from the road. You don't really need to leave the car, if you don't want to. This also includes locations that have easily accessible parking lots.

★★ A little out of the way. This is going to mean a trip down a side road, or a little walking, but you can make it, right? This may include places that are only accessible at certain times.

★★★ Park and walk over a mile. There may not be a path. There may be bugs. After all, this is North Carolina. There could be some time issues with a location being available at the right time, such as being open only a few hours a week, or seasonally.

★★★★ Expect to be tired, a little sweaty. Or cold, depending on when you go. These spots may only be accessible for a short period of time. Some people may not want you there. You may need permission to visit or at least a reservation. This is going to be a hike.

★★★★★ You'll need tools, gear, specialized equipment just to get there. You may need permission, and it may not be coming. Going could get you in serious trouble, and you probably should just avoid this unless you are allowed, and you are extremely careful. Break out the James Bond music.

Going, Going... GONE!

A note on the coordinates and lost subjects

In the past ten years, we have lost some of the subjects in the book. I left them in with updates stating they are either gone, changed, or saved in some way. I thought it was important to at least remember them. Additionally, the terminology has changed with the technology. We don't use stand alone GPS units now that most everyone has a map on a smartphone. The more accurate and current term might be map coordinates now. Either way, they still work, and most of what I originally did still applies.

The coordinates supplied are approximate, but I have tried to make them as accurate as possible. You may want to check with online maps before going to familiarize yourself with the roads and parking areas. Check to see if the subjects are still there before you go, as we have lost some over the years. They may be in dangerous areas or on private property. Do not go into any area that would be dangerous for you. This book recommends that you always get permission to enter private property before visiting or keep out.

The locations given are either on the actual spot, or in the parking area nearby. One important item about using driving maps is that they give directions based on roads. It may bring you to a location that is not optimal for parking and walking to a spot in the woods or off a road. Be familiar with the location and drive around until you find a good place to park and get out. This is why sometimes the coordinates are set for a parking area as opposed to the actual object.

Most auto GPS devices in North America will automatically put in the negative sign or the West notation for longitude. Online maps will not. When using coordinates on any computer map, use either N and W, or place a negative sign (-) by the longitude. If you do not do this, you end up in Tibet. No, really, you will.

Coastal

8 Joe Sledge

Manmade Palm Tree

Wrightsville Beach 34.22012° -77.80910°

Is it a fake metal palm tree? Maybe *real* metal palm tree would be a better name for this. Palm Tree Island first appeared in 2000, with its strange namesake ornamental palm tree sprouting up from the sand on an island just north of the bridge between Wilmington and Harbor Island. The palm tree can be either cute or curious, depending on the water level of the waterway. When the water level is low, the island is exposed and looks quaint with its lone palm. When the water is high, the island is under water and the palm tree sticks out through the water like an odd channel marker.

For a while, little seemed to be known about this piece of art placed on an island on the intracoastal waterway in Wrightsville Beach. Residents say that the palm tree is taken care of by a secret society of locals, according to an article in the Wilmington Star News. If there is any damage on "The Diminishing Republic," as the island is also known, someone would sneak over and repair the tree. But over the years, the secret got out. It is more likely that a large group of people will cruise over and party on the island for a while. Now an annual party happens on Palm Tree Island every Memorial Day weekend to celebrate the tree and do a few repairs. A tent labeled as the customs house is put up for people to sign in before they begin to party. There usually is a steel drum band rocking the island as people cruise over in their boats. The party is fun, but still family oriented, and they always leave the island cleaner than they found it.

One of the legends about the origin of the tree is that the day after a couple that lived nearby on Lee's Cut scattered the ashes of their son off the nearby point, the tree miraculously sprouted from the island. The original tree was a live one, supposedly a rare salt palm, the only one of its kind in America. Sometime during the year 2000 the live tree was replaced with the current artificial tree, secured to the island in a giant cement barrel. At the base of the tree is an inscription in cement dating the tree to 2000.

In addition to the palm tree, there is also a parking meter with an attached boat cleat on the island. The meter has an inscription from a Joni Mitchell song, which made an offhand remark referring to Wrightsville Beach installing parking meters throughout the beach area, which drew the ire of locals and Wilmington residents. Essentially, everyone had to pay to go to the beach, whether they were local or tourist. The island parking meter may be a bit of protest art, saying, "You gotta pay here, too." A thatch umbrella has also appeared on the island in recent years, giving the sandbar a slight Gilligan's Island feeling.

The palm tree is about 12 feet tall from the base to the fronds, but may appear taller or shorter depending on the water level. The island goes under water during periods of high tide, so access is limited to times of lower water levels. On occasion, people can be seen walking around the island at low tide.

Oddity ★★★★

Some of the things you'll see from this book will make you do a double take. You'll stare at this thing so much it will make you wreck on the bridge going over to Wrightsville Beach.

Difficulty ★★★★★

Under the bridge there is a boat ramp and parking area that would allow you to walk out to see the island from land. Getting on the island is a different story. I would recommend a kayak at least. And good calm weather. Remember that the island will flood and disappear at high tide. Power boats will pass by. Only go if it is safe to go there.

Fort Fisher Hermit

Fort Fisher 33.95791° -77.93031°

Robert E. Harrill made a name for himself for 17 years as the Fort Fisher Hermit, a man content to live out his life with nature, assisted by the security of an abandoned World War II era bunker on land near New Inlet at Fort Fisher, just south of Carolina Beach. He had decided to start his life over since the first 62 years of his life had been less than happy.

Born in Gaffney, SC, in 1893, Robert lost both his mother and two brothers to typhoid fever when he was young. Harrill was raised by his father and tyrannical stepmother. He was sent to live with his step-grandmother, whom he said would beat him and scream at him for any real or imagined error. Harrill would often find solace by escaping into the woods near his home, beginning his relationship with nature.

As an adult, Robert married Katie Hamrick and lived in Shelby, at the foothills of the mountains. He and his wife had four sons, as well as a daughter, Nellie Kate, who died soon after birth. Robert suffered numerous failed business ventures and held frequent low paying jobs. His marriage was increasingly rocky because of the interference of Katie's family, and, in 1935, Robert's oldest son died from a jump from a railroad trestle. Katie left soon afterwards to take a job as a housekeeper, pushing Robert over the edge. It was not long before Robert and Katie were divorced to go their separate ways.

While unsuccessful in some ways, Robert showed intelligence and ingenuity way before arriving to Fort Fisher. Years before, soon after they were married, Robert bought and modified an old Model T into a camper bus-possibly the first ever RV. He would pack up his family into the bus and take off to parts unknown, often ending up at Carolina Beach and Fort Fisher. These early visits were when he first developed a fondness for Fort Fisher, and learned it was a place where he could survive and live.

More than once, his in-laws had Robert removed to a State Hospital in Morganton "for observation". On his final visit, he fashioned a spoon into a key and escaped. Later, the employees said that no one bothered to go after him. He found his way to a lecture in Spruce Pine, NC given by Dr. William Markus Taylor. His meeting with Dr. Taylor would turn his life around and give him a new goal of earning a degree in Bio-Psychology.

In the summer of 1955, Robert decided to leave all the negative people behind and hitchhiked his way to Fort Fisher, a distance of over 290 miles. He pitched a tent by the old fort, but was locked up by a sheriff's deputy, and soon sent back home to live with his sister Mae, near Charlotte. The following summer, Robert made it back to the coast, and found more secure surroundings off the beaten path at the south end of Fort Fisher. He set up home at the bunker, which was abandoned by the Army after WWII, and this time he stayed. Harrill remained there for the next 17 years.

Over time, Robert attracted crowds of people and became known as the Fort Fisher Hermit. While not a hermit in the truest sense of the word, he was definitely clever enough to survive life in the rugged salt marsh, the harsh winters, and the fierce storms of the summer. Robert grew a vegetable garden near the bunker in order to supplement the food he gathered from the land. He caught fresh fish and crabs in the waters, and collected oysters from nearby marsh. His meals were sometimes supplemented by friends bringing leftovers, or the occasional gift of groceries.

Robert learned a lot about living off of the land by another person, a true hermit, living at Fort Fisher, named Empy Hewitt. Within a short while, Empy and Robert struck up a deep friendship. Empy would show Robert which plants to eat and how to trap fish in the marsh. He was also responsible for directing Robert to the bunker, giving him shelter, and cementing a legend in the process.

Soon, Robert became a serious tourist attraction at Fort Fisher, drawing people to Kure Beach and Carolina Beach from all over the state. People wanted to "see the hermit." During the 1960s, thousands of people would come down to see the hermit, take his picture, and talk with him. Harrill would invariably be dressed in what would become his costume, an old straw hat and swim trunks. Harrill would sometimes even change into this outfit during cold weather, in order for visitors to take back a picture with him on the sunny coast of North Carolina.

Robert had to survive difficult conditions out on the marsh, including biting flies and mosquitoes. But mosquitoes weren't the only pests that he had to suffer on occasion. Visitors would come all day during the summer months, making it hard for him to get on with his normal day to day activities. However, Robert liked having visitors. People were welcomed to sign a guestbook and donate a few coins into a nearby frying pan. His guestbook, little notebooks put out in front of the bunker, was filled with over 100,000 signatures from across the United States and many foreign countries. Robert used the money donated to buy the things he needed that he couldn't find himself. He would often hitchhike or walk to Carolina Beach in order to buy groceries from the local A&P grocery store. Locals also visited Harrill. Many of them were usually glad to help Robert clean up the bunker or help chop wood in the winter months. They loved to visit and hear about his "School of Common Sense," a discussion of his philosophies given from under the shade of a tree to anyone who would gather to listen. Carolina Beach residents would go see Robert later in the evening, visiting after the tourists were gone, roasting marshmallows and just talking.

Unfortunately, not all of the people around Kure and Carolina Beach liked the hermit. He was often the target of hooligans, sometimes out to steal money, sometimes just drunk and looking to cause trouble for the old man. He was attacked, beaten, hit with a pipe in the head, even kidnapped over his years at the bunker. He was the target of various groups who wanted him to be moved from the bunker, for one reason or another. The federal government wanted him off because he was possibly in the buffer zone for the nearby military arsenal. There were also plans to develop the land he lived on for a subdivision called Ramsgate, and Robert's home was in the middle. Robert claimed the land by Adverse Possession, and no one was able to move the hermit off his property.

The hermit could have happily lived out his life peacefully down at the bunker, but unfortunately that was not to be. While he had survived several attacks in the past, he died mysteriously in the summer of 1972. On June 1, 1972, Robert told friends who had come down to visit that some men in a Volkswagen had been out harassing him and that someone was going to kill him. The friends spent two nights with him, but on the third night the mother of one of Robert's guests caught wind and refused to let them go. Late that night, he had unwelcomed visitors.

The next day, Sunday, June 4, Ricky Norris, Jeff Barbour and some friends decided to go down to see the hermit. School had just gotten out for the summer, and they had never been down to visit the hermit before, so this seemed like a good time to go. When they arrived, they found the hermit dead in his bunker, his body strewn over wood and junk inside, and covered with sand and blood, with large boards blocking the door. The hermit's body showed fresh cuts and scrapes. The boys went back and reported their discovery to the police. Fred Pickler, the Evidence Technician and photographer with New Hanover County Sheriff's Department, as well as a longtime friend to the hermit, took pictures of the site and discovered numerous clues to the hermit's death. Pickler found an area nearby that showed a fresh disturbance in the sand. He found fresh footprints heading out toward the marsh. In the mud, Pickler saw the footprints deep in the muck, indicating they were carrying a heavy load. Near to the marsh was the hermit's sleeping bag cover, which he used as a blanket. Pickler also discovered a man's dress shoe, stuck in the mud, but still dry on the inside, indicating to him that the shoe had come off after the most recent tide change. The hermit's body was found inside the bunker, on top of broken wood and other items lying around inside. Pickler said it seemed like Robert was dumped on top of the mess inside the bunker, his body covered in sand and soaking wet. There was sand in his beard, hair, and pockets. It looked to Pickler as if Harrill had been in a serious struggle. He may have been pulled or carried in his sleeping bag toward the salt marsh, where he was beaten, and then he was tossed back into the bunker. Even though Pickler had serious concerns, the Sheriff's Department denied the need for an autopsy. The coroner and the Sheriff took the body to the morgue and cleaned it up before presenting it to the Medical Examiner. They insisted there were no signs of foul play. Believing the statements, the cause of death was listed as senile defibrillation, or basically from "natural causes". While many people suspected foul play, there was no formal investigation into his death, and his possible murderers have never been brought to trial.

Robert Harrill passed on that day, but the legend of the Fort Fisher Hermit would live on. On the 100 year anniversary of Robert Harrill's birth, in June of 1993, the Hermit Society was formed. It created a living history and gathering point for people who knew or met Robert Harrill. The Society was founded by Michael Edwards, along with Harrill's son, Edward Harrill, and Edward's wife Vergie, Harry Warren and Gaile Welker. Fred Pickler, the photographer who captured the photographic evidence after Harrill's death, is also a member, and has published a photo book of pictures he took over the years of visiting the hermit. Michael Edwards has published several books on Harrill, including *The Last Battle for Independence: The Story of the Fort Fisher Hermit*, and *Adverse*

Possessions-The Complete Story of Robert E. Harrill-The Fort Fisher Hermit. In 2004, with assistance from the Hermit Society, Rob Hill produced and directed an award winning documentary of Harrill, called "The Fort Fisher Hermit: The Life & Death of Robert E. Harrill."

The bunker still sits quietly out on the sand by the marsh. Scrub brush has grown up nearby, and the marsh has receded somewhat from Robert's time, but the look and feel is still there. Access to the bunker is best found by a walk from either the Recreation Area beach access or the NC Aquarium. The walk is a beautiful stroll through the sand, by windswept trees, and over the saltgrass covered marsh. As you amble along the walkways that bridge the marsh, you may see scuttling crabs diving for their hiding places in tiny holes in the mud as they sense your approach. The bunker itself is a solid squat concrete building. Going in the summer, with a solid foundation of mosquito repellent, you will get the feeling of what it must have been like to live through the heat of the day. While the wind whips freely across the marsh, inside the bunker it is still, hot and stuffy. You will be amazed how someone could live, and thrive, in such an environment.

Oddity ★★

The story of the life and death of Robert Harrill is beautiful and tragic, and fulfilling in the way people took up his cause after he moved on.

Difficulty ★★★★

Park at the beach access or the aquarium and follow the Hermit Trail. Be ready for a sandy hike. The days get sunny and hot in the summer, so take water. If it's still, you'll need some bug spray.

Robert Harrill was buried on the beach he loved in Federal Point cemetery. His grave is marked with seashells placed by loving locals and visitors. See it just outside the cemetery, in the old part, around 34.01790° -77.91464°.

Money Island

Wilmington 34.20188° -77.81813°

Who wouldn't enjoy a chance to pad their feet where pirate boots stomped centuries before? And not just any pirate, but Captain Kidd himself, no less.

Captain Kidd had lived the proverbial life of the swashbuckling pirate. As a privateer, he robbed ships that were the enemy of King William III, and for King William's blessing, Kidd would give one tenth of all his captured treasure back to the king. Fortunately for Kidd, business in privateering was good. It probably was a little too good, and Kidd got a bit greedy, not making his payments to the king regularly enough, then not at all.

The first loss for Captain Kidd was in losing his political support from the king. Greed will do that. The next thing that cost him was a problem sailor. Kidd whacked a swab on the head with a bucket, and the blow killed the sailor. Because of that act, Kidd was labeled a murderer.

Kidd added to his tribulations by a bit of piracy on a French vessel. Kidd was supposed to attack and pilfer from any enemy of the English crown, and the French were definitely enemies. The only issue was that, while the ship was French, the captain was an Englishman. Robbing an Englishman was a no-no for English pirates.

In order to answer for his crimes, Kidd decided to sail north, back up to New York, where he had a home and friends in government, including three governors. He buried his treasure before going to New York. He made plans that, if exonerated, he would be able to come back to get some of his treasure. If convicted, he considered using maps to his buried treasure to trade for a lessened sentence or his release.

In 1699, Kidd buried two chests laden with gold and silver on land in current Greenville Sound, leaving a shipmate, John Redfield, there to guard it. Kidd marked each spot by planting sapling trees over each chest. In order to make Redfield's life a little easier, Kidd also left goldburied along the shore for Redfield to use while he waited for Kidd to return, instructing Redfield to take from the gold stashes, as well as from one of the large iron chests if needed. Redfield build a home on the waterside to watch over the treasure, and used a sloop left for him to sail the waters to get to the various spots where the gold was buried for him.

Unfortunately for Kidd, his plans did not turn out well. Kidd was captured in England in 1700. Even after pleading with his former benefactor, William III, there was no help coming. It seems Captain Kidd had burned too many bridges in his years as a privateer. The pirate captain met his end at the end of a rope, being hanged in London for murder and piracy. Kidd's body was hung over the Thames for two years as a reminder of what happens to brigands. Pirates beware, indeed.

Redfield fared better, taking his payments and ultimately moving to Charleston SC, where he married and raised a family. Redfield lived the good life off of Kidd's gifts. He told his children tales of the captain's buried treasure, and how Kidd left the money for him to guard the treasure. As the tales were retold, the legend grew, and over the years, the story of Money Island was born.

Of course, rumor alone cannot keep a tale alive for hundreds of years. Stories abound of people finding gold coins on the shoreline, just lying in the sand. In the 1840s a descendent of Redfield dug through the wet sand and tree roots until finding an old broken chest and a few gold coins. Later, when the intercoastal waterway was cut through the island, supposedly the dredge pulled up pieces of eight from the muck. But no one knows what could still be buried on the island, or under the water.

There is one way to find treasure on Money Island. Make sure it already is there when you dig for it. Dr. George Worth did exactly that. Worth was a family friend of James Sprunt, whose family owned the island. Worth travelled the world, and during his trips home to Wilmington, Worth would create elaborate pirate maps for the children of Sprunt's family and friends. Worth would say that during his travels he had purchased or found an ancient map that showed the exact location of Kidd's treasure. He then would go over to the island early, salt the soil with trinkets and coins for the kids to find, then wait until the full moon to take the kids over for a nighttime treasure hunt they would never forget.

Money Island may still be owned by the Sprunt family. While the islands south of Masonboro Inlet are part of the Coastal Reserve, islands to the north, including Money Island, are privately owned. Because of this, trespassing is not recommended. Access to the island would be relatively easy by water, but any treasure found might rightly belong to the Sprunts. Unless Captain Kidd's ghost happens to show up.

Oddity

Yes, it's just an island, but it's a pirate island. With pirate treasure.

Difficulty

Money Island is just down from the palm tree by the Wrightsville Beach bridge. It has been bisected by the Intracoastal Waterway, so you may find some treasure on either side. You are going to need a boat to get there. And maybe a pegleg.

Price's Creek Lighthouse

Southport 33.93609° -77.98971°

North Carolina has a deserved reputation for its great lighthouses. Cape Hatteras stands tall and majestic overlooking the Graveyard of the Atlantic. Stately Currituck Light competes with Ocracoke Lighthouse for propriety of their domain, fitting in just so well with the rest of the scenery in each of their locales. Bodie Island light has slowly drifted away from its original purpose of marking the Oregon Inlet, and seems a lonely, but accessible attraction. Further down on Cape Lookout, its light is well dressed in its tuxedo diamonds. Oak Island Light is modern, clean, and bright, very bright, while across the water Old Baldy still stands, like a sea captain forced to retire, but always wanting to be back at sea.

Then there is little Price's Creek lighthouse. At 20 feet tall it is closer to a chimney than a light. It was built in 1849 as the front end of a pair of range lights for the Cape Fear River. Range lights were pairs of lights, a taller one several hundred feet upriver of the shorter one. Ship captains coming in at night would line their ship up to where the two lights would be aligned vertically to know they were in the middle of the channel. Then they were able to steam in at high speed through the deep water of the channel. This proved extremely useful to the blockade runners steaming into Wilmington during the Civil War.

Sadly, the war, storms, time and progress have taken their toll on Price's Creek Light. The taller light was dismantled after storms had damaged it beyond repair. Locals hauled the bricks away for other purposes. All that is left of the channel range lights is little Price's Creek Light, and it has seen better days. The entire lantern room, along with its Fresnel lens, is gone, and the light stands in disrepair. The light is now on private land, a citric acid plant owned by Archer Daniels Midland, and there is no public access from the plant. However, the brick tower can be seen from the ferry as it arrives and leaves the Southport docks.

Oddity ★★

While there isn't much left of the light to see, it is still the last of its kind.

Difficulty ★★★★★

Before you go, know that you are near a very strict military base, and going out on the water too close to the docks will get you an armed escort. You are probably going to need a boat (paddlers occasionally go visit the light) and permission from ADM to actually get close to this thing. But they don't give permission. I asked. And, unless something is done to preserve or restore it, you probably won't have long to see it.

Mary's Gone Wild Bottle Village

Supply 33.93474° -78.29438°

If some people get handed a poor fortune for their life, it would be understandable if they just went through the motions, doing what they need to take care of themselves. But Mary Paulsen knew there was more to her lot in life--a lot more. Even though she lost her father to the sea at age 11, she made it her point to help raise her family, taking care of the 5 youngest of her 9 siblings, making sure they had the best that she could give out of her life. When her little sister's doll broke, Mary would mend it. Soon, other girls in the neighborhood would bring their dolls to be fixed by Mary. She did her best to make sure that she and her family could have what they needed, even if they couldn't always get what they wanted. As she grew up, she continued to serve others in whatever way she could. Mary would suffer another loss as an adult, when her husband would also be lost to the ocean, passing on while collecting clams off of Bald Head Island. Mary then worked at Captain John's, a local seafood restaurant in Calabash for 25 years in order to support her own family of two children.

In 1996, Mary would get a vision from God, telling her to build a village for the doll collection she had accumulated over the years. After creating a museum for her collection, complete with little doll houses and décor, Mary received a vision to expand her collection outside the museum to all around her yard. The museum helps Mary collect donations to help provide food for hungry children.

She also helps out locals in need, buying castoff items from people in need of money for a bill or food. She then turns around and uses the recycled things to create her own version of folk art. She says that even if someone buys something from her and throws it away later, at least it is thrown away out of Brunswick County.

Mary's inspirations continued, with her building a chapel out of bottles, complete with tiny pews on the inside. Even though she had no real training in building, she knew how to design and build all the buildings on her land. Not only does she have a doll house and chapel, there also is a train depot, schoolhouse, a library, soda shop, a general store, a sailboat with a lighthouse, and a tree house. Mary was even married to her current husband Paul in her chapel in 1998.

1998 also brought Mary a new vision. She received a vision of how to paint on the reverse side of glass. Mary painted on old window panes, putting down details first, and then painting the background afterwards, essentially painting in reverse of the way painters normally create. Mary would paint the designs on the glass, not knowing what it will look like until she turns the glass over.

Her story for her first reverse painting shows the extraordinary positive happenstance of what Mary brings to life. While painting her first window, her mother and husband teased her about the work, saying she should do something that would be beneficial, something that would make money. She said she was. By ten o'clock the next morning, she had sold her first painting for eighty dollars. Her formerly skeptical family's response?

"Get her more windows."

Mary Paulsen keeps Mary's Gone Wild open every day from 9 am to 9 pm. Mary will be the lady with the red hair, the colorful outfit, the engaging personality, and the continual cheerful laugh.

Oddity ★★★★

The dollhouse can be sufficiently strange on its own, with about 6000 dolls staring vacantly at you. The whole place is amazing when you realize that it is still pretty new, and has been made only by Mary, who had no formal training in building or architecture.

Difficulty ★

With all the buildings and bottles, this place beautifully cluttered, but it also gets somewhat buggy and overgrown in the summer. Keep little ones close, or leave them at home if they have a tendency to also go wild. Mary's Gone Wild is located on Highway 130/Holden Beach Road in Supply, but her location is closer to Holden Beach. Check your rearview when you slam on the brakes at this place. Someone else may be looking at Mary's and not at the road.

Mary Paulsen uses proceeds from her sale of art to help provide food for hungry children in the US and abroad. She has a certificate for feeding over 14,000 kids in six months. She may try to hide her angel wings, but you can see them if you look just right.

Operation Bumblebee Spotting Towers

Topsail Beach

Missile Assembly Building 34.36723° -77.62968°

Control Tower 34.366428° -77.62904°

Tower   34.45401°   -77.49624°

Tower   34.39333°   -77.59295°

In the beginning of rocket and missile testing for the US, Topsail Beach was anything but quiet. In March of 1947, the Navy built and began testing ramjet engines on the coast of Topsail Island. The Navy built an assembly building for constructing the missiles, a three story control tower, and seven observation towers. The program was assigned the name Operation Bumblebee, a code name for the development and testing of ramjet technology.

Operation Bumblebee remained at Topsail Beach until it was moved to China Lake in California and later White Sands Missile Range in New Mexico. But for a year and a half, over 200 missiles were assembled and fired from the site. The base was finally closed due to unfavorable weather conditions at the Topsail site, as well as increased shipping on the Atlantic.

Today the assembly building is the Missiles and More Museum, which displays information on Operation Bumblebee, as well as natural history, Native American and pirate history. The missile rail that moved the missiles through the building still hangs in the center rafters. The launch pad where the missiles were fired is just to the beach side of the assembly building, where the Jolly Roger Inn is now. The towers are scattered throughout the island. Some have been converted into beach homes. While disguised well sometimes, if you look for the metal frame like the one on the control tower, it may help give away which houses used to be the observation towers.

Oddity ★

Operation Bumblebee was the precursor to various missile development programs, including work at Cape Canaveral and China Lake.

Difficulty ★★

Thanks to the US Navy, Topsail Island got a bridge, roads, electricity, and a place in history. Drive on over. Finding all the towers may be a little difficult if you can't recognize the original shapes. The Missiles and More museum is open only from 2-5 pm from spring to fall, and may be closed on certain days. Call ahead to make sure they are open if you plan to visit.

Did You See That? 31

Giant Alligator

Surf City 34.44603° -77.56118°

The Waves Surf and Sport store has a big alligator as its entrance. Visitors walk in through the mouth to get in the store. It certainly gets the attention of tourists heading toward Topsail Beach.

This may be the biggest gator visitors see on their trip, but not the only one. Alligators are out of the ordinary on the beach at Surf City, but they do appear on occasion. During the summer of 2009, a five foot alligator was spotted on the beach at Surf City. It later was captured in Topsail Beach and turned over to N.C. Wildlife officials.

Oddity ★★★★

The gator looks pretty happy to have tourists walk into his mouth. He is smiling, after all.

Difficulty ★

You can look to the right as you head to the beach, or listen for the kids screaming for you to stop. Either way, you'll find it.

Original Wright Brothers Monument

Kitty Hawk   36.06218° -75.70111°

You can't miss the Wright Brothers Monument, can you? The huge granite monument sits on top of Kill Devil Hill, with a big rotating beacon and spotlights shining at night. But what about the *original* Wright Brothers monument?

When visitors go to the Wright Brothers Memorial in Kill Devil Hills, near where the first flights took place, they see where Orville and Wilbur worked and lived during the cold, windy fall days and nights on the barren Outer Banks. Part of the display is a shack used by the brothers to keep warm or rest while out testing their gliders and before they flew the plane. Their shack shows how the Wrights were sleeping in the rafters with just a small wood stove heater to keep them warm on those cold days. The only food they had was canned vegetables they had to heat up on the little wood stove. It must have been a harsh life.

What is not revealed is that they also stayed in the cozy Kitty Hawk village while working on their gliders and testing their airplane. They stayed with the Tate family, living in their home, and probably getting some good Outer Banks seafood while inventing the airplane. The brothers would give the used cloth from their glider experiments to Mrs. Tate to make into shirts for her son. It may not have been as comfortable as their Ohio home, but it wasn't bad, either.

In 1928, the residents of Kitty Hawk erected their own monument in front of the house where the brothers would stay while they built their first glider to test their ideas of flight. The marker was placed in the front lawn of what was the W.J. Tate family home. The people of Kitty Hawk planned, bought and put up their original monument on their own two years before the plans for the large monument to the south were ever realized. The big monument on Kill Devil Hill was not finished until 1932.

The original marker reads

On this spot Sept 17, 1900
Wilbur Wright Began the assembly of
The Wright Brothers' First experimental
Glider Which led to
Man's conquest of the air.
Erected by Citizens of Kitty Hawk NC 1928

Oddity

This is a wonderful little find, and a great tribute from some great people to some great brothers.

Difficulty

It is a little like going back in time to see a bit of the sleepy village of Kitty Hawk, before development hit the Outer Banks. Moore Shore Road is off to the left of West Kitty Hawk Road as you drive into the village.

Did You See That? 35

Make sure you get out and read the back. Shhhh!! It's not the real marker! The original was damaged from fire and the elements. It currently is on display at the Kitty Hawk Town Hall.

36 Joe Sledge

Wright Brothers Monument Plaque

Kill Devil Hills 36.01420° -75.66794°

The Wright Brothers National Memorial has some amazing hidden history to it. There are just these things that you don't really notice until someone points them out to you. The monument on top of Kill Devil Hill is shaped like a stylized wing, with the sharp edge pointing in the same direction as the first flights. The hangar next to the Wright's shack was originally rebuilt with wood from the actual hangar they used. Only recently was it torn down and replaced with a replica after the elements finally took their toll on the wooden structure. Inside the museum there exist several original and replica pieces of Wright Brothers tools, including a replica of their wind tunnel that they used to test wing shapes for their plane, and an actual engine block from the 1903 Flyer.

One item long thought lost from the monument is a steel plaque that listed major achievements in flight from the Wright Brothers' first flight up until the design of the monument in 1930. The six-sided figure has a map of the world showing the path of many major flights done from the time of the Wrights up until the time the plaque was created. It also lists the Wrights' flights from 1903 to 1909, including the exhibition flights done in France, Italy, and Germany. It also lists other major achievements in flight, including Louis Bleriot's crossing of the English Channel and C.P. Rodgers' first cross country flight in the Wright brothers built *Vin Fiz*. Also listed are famous land and sea plane flights, including the U.S. Army 1924 round the world flight, Byrd's flight to the North Pole, and Lindbergh's 1927 Atlantic Ocean crossing. The last listing is of Sir Charles Kingsford Smith's Pacific crossing from Oakland to Brisbane.

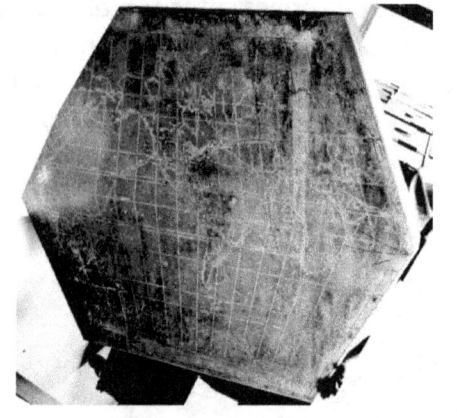

The plaque resided inside the monument for some time, hanging inside the monument until it was removed from its place on the inside wall due to water damage. Legs were attached and it was placed as a table just inside the doors of the monument. Due to the water damage causing streaks and smoothing of some of the etched parts of the map (note the rotated high contrast b&w photo for water damage and map outlines), the tablet was removed in 2010 and stored in the National Park Service archives and as of this writing is not on display. There are plans to have the plaque restored and placed back on display, either back in the monument, or in one of the display pavilions of the National Park Service.

Oddity ★

The plaque seems to have been elevated to a legendary status, as visitors to the monument from long ago remember it in their visits. Just being long missing makes it a unique item. Its ability to show a documented period of history in flight makes it very special.

Difficulty ★★★★

This could be the hardest thing to find in the book, since it's stored away and not on display as of this writing. The current coordinates go to the Wright Brothers Monument. Once it is restored, it may be as easy as going either to the museum in Kill Devil Hills to see the plaque, or you may have to see it on display in Fort Raleigh in Manteo. Or it could be placed back on the monument on the hill.

Statue of Virginia Dare

Manteo 35.93873° -75.71227°

Many people may not look twice at the marble statue of Virginia Dare hidden in the woods of the Elizabethan Gardens. Some may not even notice her as they walk into the sunken gardens, never even looking in her direction. But even if they did, even if they walk right up to her, she could never tell the amazing story of the statue, and how she arrived in the gardens.

The Virginia Dare statue was carved by Maria Louisa Lander, an American artist working in Rome in an art colony there. Lander showed a talent for sculpture early in life, and moved to Rome in her twenties to start a studio there. While in Rome, she met and befriended Nathaniel Hawthorne, a fellow native of her Salem, Massachusetts birthplace. Hawthorne commissioned Lander to carve a bust of him, one of her few works still in existence. While posing for her, Hawthorne became captivated with Lander. She eventually became the model for the free spirited women artists in his novel *The Marble Faun*.

During her time in Rome, she was involved in a scandal that caused her to be shunned by the American art society there. Rumors included stories of an affair and her posing in an improper state of undress for a fellow artist. Even though she received no more commissions, Lander would not let the rumors stop her. She continued to work, carving the

Virginia Dare statue out of a column of Carrara marble in 1859. Lander interpreted Dare as she would have looked if she had grown into adulthood, living with the local natives, and dressed as a princess in beads, with only a fishing net wrapped around her waist.

The finished statue was placed on a ship bound for America, but the vessel shipwrecked off the coast of Spain, where the sculpture stayed at the bottom of the sea. The statue was salvaged two years later, and Lander was forced to purchase her own sculpture from the salvagers. It was finally brought to Boston and displayed in an art gallery there.

The sculpture was then sold to a collector in New York for the sum of $5000. After the sculpture was delivered to the owner's studio, his building caught fire. If not for a pair of folding doors that had been closed at the time, protecting the statue from the flames, Virginia Dare may have been once again lost, for good. The purchaser of the statue died soon after the fire, and his estate refused to pay for the statue, so Virginia Dare was returned to Lander.

Lander attempted to sell the statue to the Women's Committee of the North Carolina Commission, for display in the 1893 World's Exposition in Chicago, where the state was erecting a building. With no funds available to purchase it, the Women's Committee suggested Lander donate the statue to North Carolina. By this time Lander had moved to Washington, DC, and the statue had become very close to her and she loved it greatly. She decided instead to will the statue to the state. Lander did not die until 1923, and the statue was finally accepted by North Carolina in 1926.

The statue was displayed for some time in the Hall of History in Raleigh. While the statue was exquisite and admirable, some people found the sculpture inappropriate as Virginia Dare was nude, clad only in native beads and a fishing net. Complaints came in that the statue was obscene. It also may have been that the sculpture's placement, beneath the portraits of three Confederate generals, was inappropriate as it seemed the old soldiers were leering at the naked maiden.

When the Hall of History was moved in 1938, Virginia Dare was left behind, placed in the basement of the old Supreme Court Building. For a while she was on display in the office of George Ross Pou, the state auditor, where the naked statue again dredged up some trouble. The sculpture was finally decided to be sent to Waterside Theatre, home of The Lost Colony outdoor drama.

The Lost Colony wanted nothing to do with the statue either. The sculpture was not period correct for the location, and there was no evidence that Virginia Dare had ever grown up with the natives. In fact, most believed she did not survive into adulthood. The statue was then packed away, stored in the same shipping crate she came in, in the backstage area of Waterside Theatre. Albert Q. Bell, the designer of Waterside Theatre, had the statue shipped to the home of Paul Green, the author of The Lost Colony play.

Green kept the sculpture at his home in Chapel Hill, though he never displayed it either, until the Elizabethan Gardens were created by the Roanoke Island Garden Club. He sent the statue to the gardens, where she finally found a home among the woods of her namesake's birthplace.

The sculpture is a truly lovely and amazing statue, an underappreciated piece of art in a beautiful garden. The story of the statue may overtake the sculpture itself, but the statue is still a work to behold. Some of the little items to notice on the sculpture include the regal heron, perched slightly behind her right leg, and the waves at her feet. The heron may have been a New World representation of the noble hounds placed at the feet of kings in other sculptures. The waves seem to show Virginia as pensive, looking back over the Atlantic Ocean, wondering about her family's native land of England, and who might one day come looking for her.

Oddity ★

The sculpture is nice. The story is pretty amazing.

Difficulty ★★

The Elizabethan Gardens are on the same grounds as the Lost Colony and Fort Raleigh National Historic Site, on the north side of Roanoke Island. You have to pay to get in the gardens, but it's more than worth it. The Elizabethan Gardens are a great place to take an afternoon stroll.

You may find the history of the statues, buildings, and the Gardens themselves interesting. The iron gates that are the entrance to the gatehouse? They used to be on the French Embassy in Washing ton, DC.

Silver UFO House

Frisco 35.24865° -75.60875°

Aliens haven't landed in Frisco. Well, if they did, they left their UFO behind a long time ago.

The UFO perched in Frisco is actually a unique building called a Futuro home. In 1968, Matti Suuronen, a Finnish architect, designed the Futuro home as a prefabricated metal and plastic design meant to be assembled in pieces on its final land site. The Futuro was a round, circular dome prebuilt in sections in a factory. They were either shipped to the homeowner's land and assembled there, or put together at one location and flown in completed to their final plot by helicopter. The building is designed to stand on four legs, so all the Futuro needed to be constructed was four concrete pads upon which to rest. It was meant to be the house of the future, but with rising plastic prices, the Futuro never made the impact it was meant to make. There were only about 100 Futuros ever built worldwide, and fewer than 60 are known to still exist. Frisco is the current location of one of the few Futuro homes still around. The UFO house originally sat on the west side of Highway 12, and has operated as a hot dog stand and a retail store for a while, with a day-glo green paint scheme. The Frisco UFO was repainted in shiny silver sometime in the year 2000.

It was moved to the east side of the road by the current owner. Even that has a rather curious story to it. While the Futuro was meant to be easily moved by helicopter or truck, in this case it was Hatteras islander ingenuity that got the thing moved over. Owner Leroy Reynolds got some help and lifted it onto a large flatbed truck early one morning so there would be little traffic as it moved down the road. He sat on top with a pole to move the telephone wires and got it onto its current plot of land before anyone noticed.

The UFO house sat unrepaired for a while, but due to its growing popularity, has been fixed up. The paint has been cleaned up, the interior cleaned and opened, and the outside decorated with various colorful alien artifacts. And if visitors are lucky, the alien pilot, owner Reynolds in a race suit and mask, may even show up.

Oddity ★★★

This UFO house is pure weirdness and is extremely rare.

Difficulty ★

The UFO house sits right off of Highway 12 on the ocean side of the road in between Buxton and Frisco. You won't have to get out of the car, unless they use the tractor beam on you.

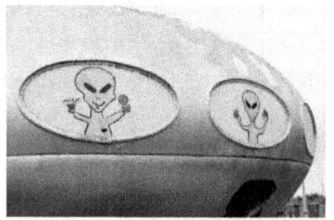

Look at the windows to find the little alien enjoying a scoop of ice cream. It's a remnant from the Futuro's snack bar days.

British Cemetery

Ocracoke 35.11668° -75.98076°

The British Cemetery in Ocracoke is a well known attraction for visitors to Ocracoke village. It is easy to find, with signs marking the way, and the street is named British Cemetery Road. But there is always a little more to every story, especially this one.

At the beginning of World War II, the US was ill prepared to protect merchant ships from Nazi U-boats in the Atlantic. Most of the U.S. fleet was being used in the Pacific to chase down and defeat the Japanese navy. At the beginning of the war, only one Navy ship was tasked with defending the Atlantic coast.

With much needed supplies going to the bottom of the sea instead of to provision strapped Great Britain, the British came to the aid of its allies with a flotilla of converted fishing trawlers, used to detect submarines, sweep for mines, attack enemy subs with deck guns and depth charges, and guide other ships to their targets, keeping the German submarines away from merchant vessels.

One of those ships was the trawler HMT *Bedfordshire*. Retasked and renamed the HMS *Bedfordshire*, the ship was armed with a 4-inch deck gun, machine gun, and depth charges. Its job was to escort and protect ships sailing Diamond Shoals by Hatteras. On May 11, 1942, the German sub U-588 torpedoed and sank the *Bedfordshire*, which went down with all hands lost. On May 14, two bodies from the *Bedfordshire* washed ashore. The bodies were identified as *Bedfordshire* sailors by Aycock Brown, whose position with the US Navy was identifying bodies found at sea and preparing them for burial.

In a strange twist, Brown was able to identify the sailors as from the *Bedfordshire* because he had talked with them only the week before. Brown had gone onboard the *Bedfordshire* in Morehead City and met with one of the officers, Sub-Lt. Thomas Cunningham. Brown had asked Cunningham for four British flags to drape over the coffins of British sailors. Cunningham gave Brown the four flags, plus two extra.

A week later, one of the bodies that Brown identified from the *Bedfordshire* would be Cunningham. Little did Cunningham know at the time that one of the two extra flags he gave Aycock Brown would have been used on his own coffin a week later. The other body was Telegraphist Stanley R. Craig. Two other bodies later recovered were never identified. The four bodies were buried in a small plot of land near Ocracoke harbor.

Originally, Ocracoke locals cared for the graves. Over the years, different groups and people have made sure the cemetery was well tended. Chief Boatswain's Mate Peter N. Stone of the U.S. Coast Guard did a lot of the care personally during his time stationed in Ocracoke as well as after he retired. Chief Stone has become an expert on the history of the *Bedfordshire* and the story of her sinking. The cemetery land was deeded to Great Britain through the Commonwealth War Graves Commission and the land is now considered British soil. The Coast Guard station and the Graveyard of the Atlantic Museum now take care of the cemetery.

All hands onboard the HMS *Bedfordshire* were lost during the torpedo attack, but there was one surviving crew member from the *Bedfordshire*. Crew member Sam Nutt missed the ship's departure at Morehead City because he had been assigned shore patrol. He wasn't released from his shore assignment until after the *Bedfordshire* departed. He boarded another British ship in order to catch up with the *Bedfordshire* at a predesignated rendezvous point and board it around Hatteras, but because the *Bedfordshire* got torpedoed, Nutt never found his ship at the rendezvous point. Since the ship was not realized to be lost for three days by anyone else, Nutt probably was the first person to realize that his ship had been sunk.

Oddity

This is a very small, and very hallowed, piece of Britain in a sleepy pirate town.

Difficulty

Go through the town and turn right on British Cemetery Road, just past the Anchorage Inn. It couldn't be any easier. You will have to catch a ferry to Ocracoke Island, and going earlier in the day will mean less waiting time at the ferry docks.

If you feel inclined to be adventurous, there is another cemetery in Buxton that holds two sailors, one unidentified, from the British merchant ship *San Delfino*.

The HMS *Bedfordshire* was only in service for two months off of Diamond Shoals before being sunk. The *Bedfordshire* had been working off the coast of Wales and even had chased off a U- Boat that was attempting to torpedo a ship that was making a repair in the Trans-Atlantic Cable.

Live Oaks

Ocracoke

Howard Oak 35.112961° -75.981248°

Springer's Point 35.105862° -75.986412°

Throughout Ocracoke, one may see live oaks, twisted, large oak trees that grow well on the sound side of the Outer Banks. The trees have low extended branches that seem like they would be perfect for hanging pirates and brigands. The trees create that great blood chilling feeling that little kids get when thinking about bloodthirsty pirates of the past meeting their end in gruesome ways.

During colonial times, English representatives would buy the oaks for exorbitant prices that even reluctant landowners could not refuse.

Then, when they had enough of the trees, they would tie the oaks together, and, rather than ship them on sailing vessels, throw them into the ocean where the Gulf Stream would carry the trees all the way across the Atlantic to hopefully wash up on the shores of England to be used to build more ships.

While many of these majestic oaks ended up as the keels of British vessels, some have survived to be preserved and honored with their own society. The Live Oak Society was founded in 1934 by Dr. Edwin Stevens to promote the preservation and recognition of the tree. Ocracoke is home to several trees in the Society, including the enormous William Howard Oak, with coordinates given here. There are others along Howard Street as well. Two more member oaks are located in Springer's Point Land Trust, a preserve located to the south of the town. One of the oaks is the appropriately named Blackbeard's Oak, after the infamous pirate who met his end at Teach's Hole off of Springer's Point.

Oddity ★

Live oaks are hauntingly beautiful, with branches that tempt kids to climb, or that, on a stormy night, may reach out to snatch passersby. Beware!

Difficulty ★★

Ocracoke is only accessible by ferry from Hatteras Island or Swan Quarter. Howard Street may be passable by car, but it is a narrow sand road, and better seen on foot. Springer's Point is accessible only by foot or bike, and has no parking at its entrance, or anywhere nearby, for that matter.

The reason why the name Howard is so prevalent on Ocracoke is because many of the residents descended from William Howard, owner of much of the island back in 1759. Howard's personal history is somewhat darker. He was quartermaster for Blackbeard from 1717 to 1718.

World's Largest Hammock (Going, going... GONE!)

Point Harbor 36.09201° -75.80755°

Who else but Nags Head Hammocks would make the world's largest hammock? In front of their store at Point Harbor in Currituck County, rests the biggest hammock ever. Actually, Nags Head Hammocks could lay claim to another world's largest, since the hammock stand is probably the biggest ever made, too.

Nags Head Hammocks says the hammock is made of almost 10,000 feet of rope, measures 42 feet long, and can hold 8,000 pounds. Yes, you can try it out, but beware running up and jumping into it. All hammocks have a tendency to tip, but this one also stretches a bit, so you may bang into the center brace of the hammock stand that is running underneath it.

Oddity ★★★

World's Longest Nap, here I come.

Difficulty ★

Nags Head Hammocks makes some great products, but something this big does occasionally need repair. It may be down to be fixed. If it is up, it would be is easy to spot on Highway 158. But it may be difficult to take home in the back of the car.

UPDATE It looks like the World's Largest Hammock is no longer there. It was taken down for repairs, but then it was never rewoven, and the store was closed. Hopefully it will be remade sometime in the future, but in the meantime, Nags Head Hammocks on the Outer Banks still has some nice chairs to sit in.

Giant Blimp Hangar

Weeksville 36.22926° -76.13538°

Prior to the US involvement in World War II, there was only one Lighter Than Air Naval Air Station on the east coast, at Lakehurst, NJ. With the great potential threat of submarines to shipping along the Outer Banks coast, the Navy commissioned and built the Weeksville Naval Air Station (LTA) to house a blimp squadron that could patrol the coast from Cape Hatteras to Norfolk, VA. Beginning in August 1941, a large steel hangar was constructed on the site, along with barracks for the air station crew, helium storage facilities, a mooring post and concrete landing pad.

The airship squadron was commissioned on April 1, 1942, and began its patrols off the coast in June of 1942, doing escort duty and search and rescue for shipping on the NC coast. The squadron continued its work on the coast until the middle of 1944, when the original air squadron was moved to North Africa and was replaced at Weeksville with another group. During this time, a second hangar was commissioned and built, an enormous wooden building that would become the largest wood structure in the world.

After WWII, the airships were decommissioned for a short time, until 1947, when airship technology began to intensify. Blimps began doing naval ship to air refueling, and formed submarine hunting groups. During its busiest time in the 1950s, the air station supported 10 blimps and 12 helicopters, as well as using the hangars for naval airplane storage. While largely meant to patrol the coast for submarines, the blimps were sometimes called upon to search for moonshine stills.

The blimp service was finally decommissioned at the end of May in 1957, after over 15 years of service. From 1957 to 1964, the field was largely abandoned, with only a small naval staff maintaining the place. The station sat empty until Westinghouse bought the property in 1966 and later spun off TCOM, Tethered Communications of Maryland, a manufacturer of blimps and aerostats. TCOM moved into airdock #2, the wooden airdock, to begin constructing and testing their blimps at the Weeksville site. The steel hangar, airdock #1, was owned by Bruce Cabinets for making kitchen and bathroom cabinets.

Sadly, on August 3, 1995, a spark from a welder's torch ignited the wooden structure of airdock # 2, burning it down to the concrete pilings. TCOM, at the time without an airdock to build their ships, bought the metal airdock #1, and is currently making airships at this site. The manufacturer makes aerostats, or tethered blimps, for private and military use, as well as airships for advertising by various companies, such as Fuji film and Metlife. During its initial flights, the Fujifilm blimp was a common site over Elizabeth City and the coast of the Outer Banks.

Oddity ★★

One of many NC superlatives, this was the home of the world's largest wooden structure.

Difficulty ★

No, you won't need to buy a blimp to get in. TCOM offers tours every Wednesday with prior notification. Call (252)330-5555 to arrange a tour. The remnants of airdock #2 are off limits to visitors, but you can see the hangars from the road.

The airship Pink Floyd, an airship built for the band's 1994 tour, was painted at the Weeksville site. Unfortunately after the tour, when the blimp was brought back to TCOM, it was destroyed during a freak thunderstorm. They should have gone with a giant pig.

Floating Church

Swan Quarter 35.40780° -76.32835°

What makes the best legends? The best ones are those that are totally amazing, utterly unbelievable, and completely true. The Church Moved by the Hand of God is just that.

Back in 1876, the Methodist residents of Swan Quarter decided to build a permanent building to hold their services. Swan Quarter, a low lying coastal town, was prone to flooding, so the church members looked for higher land on which to build. They found the perfect spot, a high and dry piece of land owned by Samuel Sadler. The only problem was Sadler wouldn't sell.

The church members found another plot of land in the village and constructed their church there. Three days after the dedication, on September 16, 1876, a huge hurricane hit the coast of NC. Coastal flooding, heavy rains, and high winds pounded Swan Quarter, flooding the town. Caught in the flood, the new church floated off its foundation and drifted up the street, where it collided with the general store, then proceeded to make a sharp right hand turn. It floated up Main Street, right to the plot of land the church members wanted to buy. As if that wasn't enough, the church then turned on its axis so that the door faced

Main Street, and settled right on that spot.

After considering the miracle that had happened, Sadler decided that the church deserved the land. The congregation got the deed for the property in 1881. One story says that Sadler saw the light and gave them the property for free. That may or may not be true, but who would blame Sadler if he did? The congregation built a brick structure in 1913 and the original floating church was used as a barn for a while. It was returned to the site in 1941 and is now used for classroom space for the church. It can be seen any time, but Sundays might be best.

Oddity

There are quite few churches with the name Providence, but you have to admit this one really deserves it.

Difficulty ★

The original floating church is right behind the brick church, at the intersection of Church St. and Main St. The congregation welcomes guests for Sunday service. And since they are Methodists, they probably will have some good food afterwards.

Belhaven Museum

Belhaven 35.53899° -76.62167°

One could probably write a book just on the things people see in the Belhaven museum. Heck, you could probably write a book on the button collection alone. Arthur Congleton, curator of the museum, referred to it as a combination of the Smithsonian Institute and Ripley's Believe It or Not.

Eva Blount Way started collecting her buttons and pins at seventeen years old, when she got married in 1887, with a gift of four buttons from her new mother-in-law. Her collection grew as she gathered things to show her grandchildren when they visited, as well as when she just found something interesting. She never stopped collecting buttons or anything else, and people kept giving her things, for decades since.

Miss Eva ultimately collected over 10,000 objects, not counting the buttons, first showcasing them in her house, where she would accept donations for the American Red Cross from her visitors. When the collection outgrew her home, she moved the collection to her barn. When she passed away in 1962 at the age of 93, the town bought her collection and moved everything to the second floor of the Belhaven town hall. The collection opened on April 1, 1965 with the official name of the Belhaven Memorial Museum, but has gained the more loving moniker, Granny's Attic.

What are some of the items a visitor can see in Granny's Attic? Well, aside from the 30,000 buttons? The museum has a pickelhaube, one of those old German/Prussian helmets with the spike on top. There is the replacement helmet, a stahlhelm, or coal scuttle helmet, to match, as well as a Maxim machine gun. There is a copy of the New York Herald, April 15, 1865, which records the information of and reaction to Abraham Lincoln's assassination, an early Kodak box camera, a collection of license plates, Confederate currency, and stereoscope pictures and viewer, which is a sort of turn of the century Viewmaster.

What else? Many of Mrs. Way's canned preserves are still in the museum. Next to the peas and okra you may find possum and potatoes. Together. Mmmmm, mmmmm!

Miss Eva was not only a great collector, she was well known for her snake killing ability, having racked up about 240 dead rattlers and other types of snakes. What is less known is what she did with them. Miss Eva, after killing the snakes, would often dissect them, to see how they worked, their anatomy, what they ate. She even had science classes over to observe her amateur lectures on ophiology (the study of snakes).

One snake gave her enough fits that she had to use more devious methods of dispatch than the sharp end of a hoe to be rid of the slithering critter. This snake had been stealing eggs from her hen house, so Miss Eva placed wooden eggs in the coop instead. The snake swallowed the egg, but could not crush it and digest the insides. The wooden egg stuck in the snake's abdomen, plugging him up and killing him. Yes, the snake perished of indigestion. You can see the snake on display at the museum.

Miss Eva got much of her collection from people donating or giving her items they found that she might like. Eva probably never knew just who would stop by to give her something. One of the museum's most looked at items came from a traveling band of gypsies who left a married couple to stay with Eva when they left. They left with her a married couple of fleas, in white dress and tuxedo.

Another story tells of how Miss Eva got a pair of fossilized walrus tusks from a Swedish sea captain. On his last journey as a captain, he docked his ship in Pantego Creek, and rowed ashore to find Miss Eva and her collection. He told her that he was on his way back home to retire. He wanted her to have his prized possession of two ancient walrus tusks to display in her collection. After giving them to Miss Eva, he got back on his ship and steamed away, never being heard from again.

There are also 19th century copying machines, uniforms, old phonographs, typewriters, and much more. Miss Eva even had a human skeleton from a doctor at Trinity College, now Duke University. The museum is open from 1 to 5 every day except Wednesdays, on the second floor of the old town hall. Admittance is free, but they do take donations. Miss Eva would want it that way.

And the best button? An Eisenhower/Nixon pin that says, "Let's Clean House With Ike and Dick."

Oddity ★★★★

I'm not sure what the dress code is for the flea wedding, or where they are registered.

Difficulty ★

Belhaven is located on US 264, and the museum is on 264 Business, in the old town hall, with parking right next to the building. It doesn't get much easier to find when the address is "Main Street."

Dugout Canoe Shipwrecks

Lake Phelps 35.78579° -76.51796°

Pettigrew State Park 35.79198° -76.40938°

Yes, there are shipwrecks in Lake Phelps.

Lake Phelps is a beautiful, nearly circular recreational lake with wonderful camping and an amazing amount of history. Way before it was home to Somerset Plantation, natives had used the lake and surrounding land for millennia as a place to hunt for food and game. Native tribes would travel to the lake, staying there long enough to hunt and fish along the shore. While there, they would make dugout canoes and pottery. When time came to move on to other land, instead of taking their canoes with them, the natives would leave the heavy, long canoes in place, to be discovered centuries later.

In the spring of 1985, a large forest fire nearby was fought with water from Lake Phelps, resulting in an abnormally low water level. That, combined with a dry summer, left Lake Phelps at an unusually depleted level. Fishermen soon started reporting pottery shards in the water, and by fall, dugout canoes were being found sunk on the edges of the clear, shallow lake.

Twenty three of the canoes have been studied, including doing radiocarbon dating. Some canoes date back to 2400 BC, with dates up to 1400 AD. The longest canoe discovered was an incredible 36 feet. The canoes survive in the lake due to the naturally acidic nature of the water, in which few decomposers can live. Two of the canoes have been pulled for display at Pettigrew State Park. Due to their age, they may not be exhibited at all times, and may  be being restored off site. The state park often has reproductions and demonstrations of how dugout canoes are made. Others can be seen in the lake, including at a public dock on the western side of the lake, though some downed trees may look like submerged canoes. The ability to see these shipwrecks will vary greatly based on the amount of waves, sun, and clarity of the water. Sunny, calm days are best.

Oddity ★

The lake itself is rather odd. Almost perfectly round and shallow, no one is quite sure how the lake formed.

Difficulty ★

This is about a 30 minute trip each way from Columbia. If you are heading to or from the Outer Banks, it is worth the side trip. Check out

Somerset Place while you are there. Remember that seeing the shipwrecks in the water is dependent on the weather and clarity of the water at the time.

Lake Phelps could have been called Lake Tarkington. Josiah Phelps and Benjamin Tarkington were hunting and searching for farmland in 1755. When they became discouraged, Tarkington climbed a tree and spotted the lake. Phelps ran ahead of Tarkington, straight into the lake. Since he got there first, Phelps got the honor of naming it.

Lake Phelps could have been called Lake Tarkington. Josiah Phelps and Benjamin Tarkington were hunting and searching for farmland in 1755. When they became discouraged, Tarkington climbed a tree and spotted the lake. Phelps ran ahead of Tarkington, straight into the lake. Since he got there first, Phelps got the honor of naming it.

Large-mouth bass are found in Lake Phelps, despite the fact that they should not be able to reproduce in acidic water of the lake. How they are able to survive is a mystery..

Ram Albemarle

Plymouth 35.86914° -76.74833°

The CSS *Albemarle* was built in response to the success of the CSS *Virginia*'s success in the Battle of Hampton Roads. The Union army had occupied much of the coastal area of North Carolina, supported by Union gunboats throughout the rivers and sounds. The *Albemarle* was meant to go down the Roanoke River and rid the waters of the gunboats so that Confederate troops could take the forts on the Roanoke. The *Albemarle* was built on the banks of the Roanoke in the area called Edward's Ferry, near Scotland Neck. It was seen as a safe place to build the ship because the Union ships could not come that far up the shallow river. The Union army found out about the ship being built in Scotland Neck, but did not spare the men to attempt an overland attack to destroy it while being built.

Big mistake on their part.

The mission of the *Albemarle* was to steam toward Plymouth and attack the ships there, taking out the ship support for the ground troops stationed at Plymouth. The Union army knew of the *Albemarle* and the massive threat it posed. Union troops built a large fort on the river near Plymouth (where the paper mill currently stands) with the sole purpose of shelling the massive gunboat to keep it out of the Union controlled waters and coastal lands. Amazingly, after first sizing up barriers in the water as being no threat to their passage, the *Albemarle* was able to steam right past the Plymouth fort unnoticed, without the soldiers firing a shot. After passing safely by Union forts, and protected by the ship's armor, the *Albemarle* came across two steamers for the Union, the USS *Miami* and the USS *Southfield*. The two Union gunboats had lashed themselves together with spars and rope, hoping to force the *Albemarle* in between them, trapping the Confederate ship. Captain James Cooke, skipper of the *Albemarle*, turned to starboard and was able to pass in the shallow water on the south bank. Then Cooke turned hard into the *Southfield*, ramming her and sinking the ship. The ram of the *Albemarle* was wedged into the *Southfield*, and as the *Southfield* sank, it began to pull the *Albemarle* under with her. The *Southfield* rolled while sinking, which freed the *Albemarle*.

While the *Albemarle* was entangled with the *Southfield*, the *Miami* fired a shot pointblank at the *Albemarle*'s armor. The shell bounced harmlessly off the side of the *Albemarle* and exploded on the *Miami*, killing its captain, Charles Flusser. Seamen from the *Miami* tried to storm the Albemarle to capture it, but were driven off by vicious musket fire from inside the ship. The *Miami* then escaped into the open waters of the Albemarle Sound.

With the Roanoke cleared of Union ships, Confederate General Robert Hoke was able to advance toward Plymouth and capture the forts and town.

The *Albemarle* would see more action on the Roanoke. When escorting a troop carrying ship, the *Albemarle*, along with the CSS *Bombshell*, a wooden sided steamer, would encounter the *Miami* again, along with the USS *Mattabesett*, USS *Sassacus*, and USS *Wyalusing*. The *Albemarle* absorbed all the shells shot at her, all the while firing on the *Mattabesett*. The *Sassacus* attempted to ram the *Albemarle* with her bronze ram. The Union ship ended up embedded on the *Albemarle*. Realizing that the *Sassacus* was at point blank range, the *Albemarle* fired two shots through the *Sassacus*' hull, puncturing her boilers. The *Sassacus* was still able to steam away, with the Union expending over 500 shells at the *Albemarle* with no discernible effect. The *Albemarle* steamed back to Plymouth unscathed.

The plans for the *Albemarle* and her sister ship, the *Neuse*, were for both ships to clear their respective rivers, then meet to shell Union occupied New Bern in support of a Confederate land attack to retake the town. While the *Albemarle* held up her end, the *Neuse*, unfortunately for the Confederates, had other plans.

The *Albemarle* owned the Roanoke River by the summer of 1864, and the Union decided that something had to be done about the ship. The accepted plan was put forth by Lieutenant William Cushing. His plan involved taking two small skiffs with spar mounted torpedoes up the Roanoke River under the cover of night and detonating the charges against the *Albemarle*. One skiff was lost on the way down from New York, but Cushing continued with his plan.

After slipping up the river and past Confederate sentries, Cushing was able to get to the dock holding the *Albemarle*. At this time, two things happened that threw his plans into disarray. He and his troops were discovered, and he found that the *Albemarle* was surrounded by floating logs to keep this type of attack from succeeding. Under fire, Cushing discovered that the logs had been in the water for a long time, and were quite slippery. His skiff slid easily over the logs. With the spar mounted torpedo firmly up against the *Albemarle*, Cushing detonated the charge.

The resulting explosion blasted Cushing back into the water. Though dazed, Cushing then swam to the side of the river and stripped off his soaked uniform. He hid there until the next day, when he stole a small boat and paddled his way back out the river to Union forces at the mouth of the Roanoke. Of all of Cushing's men, only one other escaped.

Cushing's escape was extremely perilous, but his mission had the desired consequence. Cushing had blown a hole in the *Albemarle* "big enough to drive a wagon in." She sank in six feet of water on the spot.

The ship was raised after the war, taken to New York and repaired. The ship saw little service and was later sold, probably for scrap, as no record exists of her service after the sale date.

Today you can see a replica of the *Albemarle* at the Port

O'Plymouth museum on the waterfront in Plymouth. It is a scale replica, only 63 feet compared to the original's 158 feet. It is powered and capable of sailing up the river. You can see it in action in the summer at noon each day, cruising and firing its two guns, as well as during the living history weekend at Plymouth, held around the end of April or beginning of May.

Oddity ★★★

Save that Confederate money! There's still one ship left in the navy.

Difficulty ★

Plymouth has a beautiful downtown on its waterfront. Drive right up to the museum on East Water Street.

Though the patent office may disagree, there are historical sources that say that Peter E. Smith, a farmer from Scotland Neck where the *Albemarle* was being built, invented the twist drill in order to cut down on the time it took to drill through the metal plate for the ship.

From nearly the beginning of the Civil War, the Union controlled most of coastal North Carolina solely because they could control the navigable rivers and dominate the water with their large naval presence. The reason why the rest of North Carolina was left relatively unscathed by the war was that the roads in North Carolina were so bad, it was nearly impossible to move troops along them.

CSS Neuse & CSS Neuse II

Kinston

Neuse 35.26051° -77.58171°

Neuse II 35.26137° -77.58306°

The CSS *Neuse* and the CSS *Albemarle* were the first of several planned ironclad river gunboats built for the Confederates during the early parts of the Civil War. The original CSS *Neuse* was constructed in the small town of White Hall, now the small town of Seven Springs, on the banks of the Neuse River. The *Neuse* was ordered at the same time as the *Albemarle*, its sister ship on North Carolina's rivers. And its birth was truly a baptism of fire.

One of the biggest obstacles to building the *Neuse* was the defense of the ship while under construction. This important concern became very real in December 1862, when Union troops went on a raid from New Bern into Goldsboro. The troops first ransacked Kinston, and then arrived on the south bank of the Neuse River near White Hall. The Union soldiers saw the hull of the ship and, realizing the important threat the ship would become, knew that they needed to destroy it. In order to keep the advancing Union soldiers from crossing the Neuse River, defending Confederates set fire to the White Hall Bridge crossing using turpentine and rosin that was to be used for the boat. The Union forces torched supplies on the south side of the river, too, lighting up the area for miles, and exposing the Confederates under the blazing light of the fire.

Knowing that they needed to destroy the hull of the ship before it was finished, Union troops planned to send someone over the river to attempt to burn the hull. One Union soldier volunteered to cross over the river and set fire to the gunboat.

Undressed, Private Henry Butler swam across the cold river (this was in December) and tried to set fire to the boat. Confederate soldiers realized when Butler grabbed a burning piece of the bridge in order to use it as a torch that it was his intention to set the boat ablaze. The Confederates came out from hiding places along the bank and attempted to stop Butler. With rifle shot whizzing by him, Private Butler realized the immense danger he was in and quickly plunged back into the water. After Butler was chased back to the far bank by Confederate forces, the Union troops decided to shell the riverboat to pieces with their artillery. Artillery pummeled the hull with canister shot, trying to blast it to bits. Thinking they had succeeded in severely damaging the boat, the Union forces continued on to Goldsboro.

The *Neuse* wasn't severely damaged, however, and work continued, though delayed, until the ship's hull was completed in March of 1863. The ship was moved to Kinston where armor and machinery could be lowered from the riverbank. During this time there were usual delays in procuring the iron for armor on the ship, and the delays cost the Confederacy in their ability to seize New Bern from the occupying Union troops. The continual lack of iron and delayed shipments of armor left the *Neuse* unused until April 1864.

The Confederates' plan was that the *Neuse* and the *Albemarle* would both steam to New Bern, meeting there in an attempt to take back the town. Unfortunately for the Confederates, when the *Neuse* finally steamed out of its port, the ship had barely gone a half of a mile when it grounded on a sandbar.

After the grounding the *Neuse* was stranded for a month, never getting a chance to attack New Bern. By this time most soldiers had been diverted to other fronts when General Grant began his buildup to a major push on Lee. This included a loss of Confederate ground troops to support any river excursions to free New Bern. The increased Union threat from the fall of Fort Fisher and Wilmington led the Confederates to have to scuttle the CSS *Neuse*. The ship was unable to steam without any support, and the increased number of Union soldiers in New Bern kept pressure on the ship's crew not to be able to take the ship onto the river. By 1865, the massive Union armies in North Carolina pushed past Wilmington and Goldsboro, into Kinston. Under orders, the crew of the *Neuse* fired a few shots at the approaching infantry, and then scuttled the ship. The crew of the *Neuse* set the ship ablaze, an immense explosion occurred on the bow, and the CSS *Neuse* settled into the shallow water.

From all this the unfortunate *Neuse* had even acquired, from one of its officers, Lieutenant Richard Bacot, a rather appropriate nickname. After delays, battles to get the ship built, scarcity of iron, its stranding, and the inability to get the ship into the fight, he dubbed it the *Neuse'ance*.

But even with all the problems the ship had, that wasn't the end of the *Neuse*. Since it sat in shallow waters, parts of the hull of the ship were often visible when the river was low. The area of the river became known as Gunboat Bend. In the 1930s Henry Clay Casey, a local Kinston kid, poked around in the old wreck, not knowing how big the ship really was. It wasn't until the 1950s, when some locals found some live shells left from the guns of the *Neuse*, that Casey's interest in the ship was rejuvenated. By 1961, Casey had contracted with two other men, Lemuel Houston and Thomas Carlyle, to create a salvage operation for the *Neuse*. They didn't know how big the ship was; the group assumed that they would simply use a drag line to excavate the sand and pull the hull to the shore. They figured it would take two weeks.

A month later, little progress had been made in excavating the ship, but it had garnered a lot of attention. With the centennial of the Civil War occurring, the state became involved, realizing that what Kinston had was a valuable relic, a relatively undamaged ironclad.

Unfortunately, the *Neuse'ance* had other plans. The ship was under multiple claims of ownership. Casey and his group assumed that they, as the salvagers, owned the ship, while Kinston, the federal government, and later on, the owner of the land nearby, all could have laid claims. Also, every time the river rose, the ship would sink back into the muck. It wouldn't be until the spring of 1963 that the ship would be freed from the river. The *Neuse* was fairly intact, but the summer sun would take its toll on the decking, warping, drying out, and decaying the planks. The hull would have to be cut into three sections because it was too heavy to move in one piece to its new location. By May of 1964, the *Neuse* had finally been moved to the new site at Caswell Park. By 1969, an enormous shelter had been erected to protect the remains of the *Neuse*. Even that wasn't enough, when, in 1996,

Hurricane Fran caused flooding in the area of the *Neuse*, damaging the remains of the ship. The ship was again moved to higher ground, but the visitor center was later damaged from flooding by subsequent hurricanes.

After all that, the *Neuse* still is making waves. A group in Kinston has built a land based replica of the *Neuse*. Shipbuilder Alton Stapleford began work in 2002 and finished the ship seven years later. The ship, a full sized replica, is open for tours on Saturdays, with free admission, though donations are encouraged. Visitors may even get to see groups getting trained into being naval cadets for the ship. The *Neuse II* is the only full size replica of a Confederate ship in existence.

In 2014, the original *Neuse* was moved to a permanent museum in Kinston across the street from the *Neuse II*. It is now located inside the CSS Neuse Civil War Interpretative Center. The center is open Tuesday through Saturday, and includes a framework representation of what the *Neuse* looked like when the ship was complete.

Oddity ★★★

Sure, people have boats sitting in their front yards, but this is ridiculous.

Difficulty ★

How can you miss a 185 foot ironclad gunship sporting Confederate Navy flags? It sits at the corner of Heritage and Gordon streets in downtown Kinston.

Self Kicking Machines (Going, going... gone!)

New Bern & Raleigh

34.97172° -76.97279° –East of New Bern

35.89873° -78.76429° –Raleigh

Tom Haywood freely gave out what many people really need. A swift kick in the butt.

In 1937, feeling the need for some forced inspiration or chastisement for some error, he and handyman Wilbur Herring built a self-kicking machine. The simple design allowed Tom to bend over to turn a crank, which worked a set of pulleys and belt to turn a wheel, dressed with four boots. The boots would spin on the wheel and give him a good kick in the pants.

Tom kept the machine behind his house. He only meant it for personal use. But soon people heard about it, and Tom would start to hear his machine being used late at night in his back yard. Tom moved the kicking machine to the front of his general store, where people coming home from the beach would stop and receive a dose of its medicine.

Tom and tourists weren't the only people to use the kicking machine. After Tom demonstrated it for a newsreel film, the machine became more and more popular, gaining national attention over time. The list of guests getting a kick in the backside is said to include several NC governors, a baron and baroness of Bern, Switzerland, and actress Lucille Ball.

The Haywood family ran the store and tended to the machine into the 1980s. With Highway 70 becoming a fast moving four lane, fewer people were stopping at his shop and the kicking machine got less attention later on from travelers. In 1993, the original machine was donated to the North Carolina Museum of History.

Of course, you can't keep a good oddity down. The general store became an antique store, Martha's Favorite Things, and the legend of the self-kicking machine meant that the new owner had an identical replica built on the site.

But what about people not on the coast? Are folks from the Piedmont immune from needing a swift kick in the pants? No, location doesn't matter. Nor does affluence, it seems. The Angus Barn Restaurant in Raleigh has a self kicking machine in the back parking lot. This one, while serving up the same dose of kick yourself in the backside, is considered a little tougher, as it works entirely on a gear system, so there is less give when you receive the kick. Hopefully you took some pleasure the meal if you receive some pain in the backside later on.

Oddity

There should be more of these things. They give out something that everyone needs.

Difficulty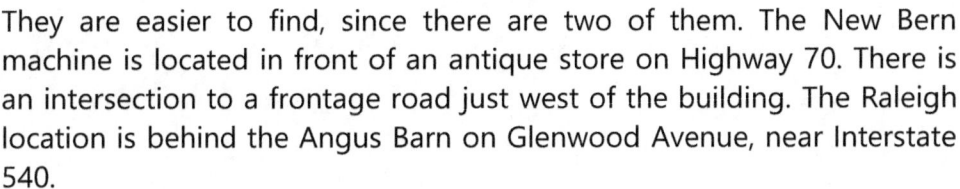

They are easier to find, since there are two of them. The New Bern machine is located in front of an antique store on Highway 70. There is an intersection to a frontage road just west of the building. The Raleigh location is behind the Angus Barn on Glenwood Avenue, near Interstate 540.

UPDATE So, the very first, original kick yerself in the butt machine was placed in the NC Museum of History, and a replica was put in its place outside of New Bern, but when that store closed down, the replica was removed. There is nothing there anymore, though the one in Raleigh is still working.

Mysterious Hoofprints

Bath 35.50864° -76.90580°

Quiet sleepy Bath doesn't seem like a town with a curse on it. Not now, anyway.

What used to be the first town in North Carolina, as well as its first port, and nominal colonial capital, is now a beautiful little town of less than 300 inhabitants. But what a history this place has had.

Indian wars, disease, rebellion, and the residency of a famous pirate took its toll on the town. George Whitefield, a famous traveling evangelist, cursed the town when he was not able to stop the continual drinking and wildness. He shook the dust from his shoes and placed a curse on the town for a hundred years.

You'd think residents would have learned their lesson when Bath faded into obscurity as nearby Washington grew into the major port of the area. But it seems someone didn't take the hint. One resident was pretty notorious for his rowdy shenanigans. Jessie Elliot was well known for his hard drinking ways. He and some of his cronies would often spend the Sabbath not only drinking  and swearing, but horseracing for money as well. A big no-no on Sunday.

Jessie was pretty famous for having a fast horse. It was so good that Jessie felt no one could beat him. One Sunday morning in October, 1813, with Jessie bragging about his horse being the fastest in the county, a stranger met Jessie and threw down the challenge that Jessie's horse could be beaten. A wager of one hundred dollars was placed on the race. Jessie, always up for a challenge, accepted the bet on the spot.

An hour later, Jessie met the stranger at the race track. The dark stranger was eerily calm before the race, which set Jessie off a bit, but liquid courage had steeled his resolve. The race started, and Jessie quickly found himself in the lead. Jessie urged his horse on. Jessie's horse continued to increase the distance between him and the stranger. Jessie, feeling his confidence, yelled, "Take me in a winner, or take me to Hell!"

At that very moment, Jessie's horse, at the utterance of those words, stopped in its tracks, embedding its hoofs in the soft earth. Jessie kept going. He flipped over the horse's head, slamming into a pine tree, killing him instantly. The dark stranger dismounted his black horse and knelt beside the lifeless body of Jessie Elliot, then climbed back upon his own steed and disappeared into the woods, not collecting his winnings. He had gotten what he really came for.

No one really can say if the Devil raced Jessie for his soul that day and collected on the wager. But the horse's hoof prints remained. Since 1813, the hoof prints have been embedded in the soil, marking the point where the horse stopped and Jessie Elliot flew out of the saddle, plowing into a tree trunk and dying. Locals told of the story, explaining that the footprints endured as a lasting reminder of what happens to any sinner run amok in Bath.

The legend of the prints stated that nothing would grow in the indentations. Nothing, no dirt, no stick or leaf, would stay inside the prints. Kids on their way to school would place leaves and twigs in the prints, only to find them empty on the way home.

A newsreel cameraman named Earl Harrell heard of the legend and came to get pictures of the legendary prints. A farmer told him that neither chickens nor pigs would eat corn feed inside the prints. Harrell even tried the experiment himself. He found that chickens would eat the feed all around the prints, but wouldn't touch anything inside the impressions. Harrell even concocted a net of string over the prints after placing leaves, dirt and rocks inside. The next day, the prints were empty. The string was undisturbed.

The hoof prints have long been a roadside stop for explorers of the unexplained. The area used to be wooded, but the trees have been cut down and the area has gone to weed. The footprints are still there, though, and nothing stays in them. Grass overgrows around the footprints, obscuring them somewhat, but the grass doesn't grow inside.

The hoof prints are on private property, in a weedy, bushy area, with a small cable fence marking their place. There really is no place nearby to pull off the road easily, except for a small dirt path on the left. The owners may or may not mind you visiting, so do your best to be respectful. Remember what happened to Jessie Elliot.

Oddity ★★★★

It's amazing enough that the hoof prints have remained for all these years. There are stories of locals making fake hoof prints to fool visitors, or even of people trying to dig them up. The mysterious hoof prints still remain. If you find them, and if you have the time, try it out. Put something in the hoof prints, then spend the day tracking Blackbeard in Bath. Come back and see if the hoof prints are still cursed.

Difficulty ★★

The footprints are about 1/3 of a mile down on Camp Leach Rd, off of NC 92. These are only fifty feet off the road and to the left, but there is a lot of overgrowth. The remnants of a concrete pad once used for a concession stand have been used as a marker to find where to walk into the weeds, but on a recent visit, the pad was not noticeable. No matter what, be aware that you may not be welcome by the owners, the neighbors, the dogs, or the bugs and ticks. The hoof prints are on private property, so get permission before looking. And don't race there, no matter what you do!

Some stories tell that there are more than the four hoof prints. There may be eight or more, either from Jessie's horse stumbling to a stop, or from the mysterious dark rider who stopped at Jessie's dead body.

Maco Light

Maco 34.27619° -78.12392°

The story of Maco Light often makes short work of the cause of the light, which was the death of Joe Baldwin, a conductor on the train that ran into Wilmington during the 1800s. Most of the legend focuses on the tale of the light, not on Joe himself, which is too bad. Joe did a truly heroic act. How many other people would be so dedicated as to give their own life trying to warn an approaching train of danger?

Back in 1867, Joe Baldwin worked for the Wilmington, Manchester and Augusta Railroad. His job normally was to announce the towns they were approaching to the passengers. Around Maco, when he got up to announce their impending arrival to Wilmington, he noticed that the caboose he was riding in had suddenly become detached from the rest of the train. Rapidly slowing, the car would be dead on the rails, in the dark, with a high speed express due to be quickly charging up behind him.

Joe grabbed his lantern and began frantically waving his signal, trying to warn the approaching train that the tracks were blocked. Joe's attempt was futile, however, and the approaching train plowed into Joe's car. The other train derailed, but no one on it was injured. Joe was not so fortunate. The terrible impact severed Joe's head from his body, and tossed the lantern into the swamp. Joe's body was discovered near the wreck, but without his head. People searched the area for days for poor Joe's head, but it was never found. Joe was later buried, headless, in a Wilmington graveyard.

Soon after the accident, a couple, strolling near the Maco station, reported seeing a strange floating light nearby. That was the beginning of the legend of Maco Light. For over a hundred years, people would report seeing the ghostly lantern floating down the tracks. The light was so prevalent that trains were seeing it as they passed Maco. The railroad had to start using two lights, one red and one green, for trains running to Wilmington, so they wouldn't confuse the Maco light with real signal lights from other trains. President Grover Cleveland, on a stop in Wilmington, asked about the two signal lights and was told of the legend of Maco light. Some stories even say that President Cleveland may have seen the light himself. Partly due to President Cleveland's interest, the light became nationally known and over time became highly visited. Many visitors to the Wilmington coast would often visit the light. The light appeared so frequently and regularly that it was less a question of if one would see the light, but more of how well the light would appear.

The light had been pursued and analyzed by many groups, including an army colonel with troops who surrounded the light, only to have it disappear and reappear behind them. Several stories tell of people being chased by the light or people chasing it with nets in hope of capturing the light.

One rather interesting sidebar to this tale is that there are no actual records of a train crash in 1867, and no one named Joe Baldwin either worked for the railroad or died back then. There is a story of a man named Charles Baldwin, possibly nicknamed Joe, who died in an accident near where Maco is now, but did not lose his head, and he was not on a train. It could be that this is really Charles Baldwin walking the tracks. One story that lends credence to this is that in 1965, Hans Holzer, a famous paranormal investigator, studied the light and said that Joe Baldwin actually was not looking for his head, but instead did not realize he had passed on. He was still trying to signal the other train. He was still just trying to do his job.

Sadly, the tracks were abandoned and later pulled up in 1977, and the Maco Light disappeared. Outside of one photograph by N.C.H.A.G.S., a paranormal investigation group, no one has seen anything from the light since the tracks were removed. Most figure Joe realized that without the tracks for trains to run, his job was finally finished. Rest in peace, Joe.

Oddity

If half of the stories are true, this must have been a great sight to see.

Difficulty ★★★★

Do not kid yourself on this one. Not only is the area hard to find, it is illegal and unwanted for people to go exploring for this light. Most locals won't talk about it. The old depot is not there, and some of the remnants of the rail line are under water in the swamp. The two roads in the area that lead to the train track remnants may be public, but that doesn't mean you will be welcome. As a matter of fact, the coordinates will only take you to the end of one public road, and I wouldn't go any farther. If you go without getting permission from the owners of the property, the likelihood is extremely high that you will get charged with trespassing (or attacked by a dog). Oh yeah, the light is not there anymore, anyway.

Charles Baldwin (not Joe) was buried, with his head attached, in Wilmington. Later, his grave was moved, but when the gravediggers went back for the marker, they forgot where he was buried. Charles now rests in an unmarked grave somewhere in Wilmington.

Nancy Roberts was one of the most famous collectors of American folklore. She and her husband Bruce took an epic photo of the Maco Light that showed the light floating over the tracks with lightning flashing in the background.

World's Largest Frying Pan

Rose Hill 34.82633° -78.02191°

Built in 1963 to recognize the chicken industry, the world's largest frying pan sits under a large red roof in Rose Hill. It has been used for chicken cookouts, fundraisers, and promotion of the poultry farming in eastern NC. The frying pan originally was made in several wedge shapes and assembled for the festivals, but now it is permanently set up in the park at Rose Hill. It is powered by 40 gas burners and can hold 365 chickens on its 15 foot diameter pan.

You can tell this thing is still used, as some would say the pan is well seasoned. Others might say it is greasy and smelly. But that's part of what gives it character. Dibs on the thigh.

There are other frying pans out there claiming to be the world's largest, but none have the diameter of Rose Hill's. Some are not used as frying pans, and one is not even iron!

Oddity ★★

It probably is pretty impressive when it's working... And you are hungry.

Difficulty ★

Turn off of I-40 and it is right down Sycamore Street. The town even has signs for it.

Brady C. Jefcoat Museum of Americana

Murfreesboro 36.44019° -77.10231°

What is the Brady Jefcoat Museum's claim to fame? It is the repository of the world's largest collection of washing machines, flat irons, and dairy equipment. If that's not enough, the rest of the 13,000 items will intrigue, or at least distract, the guests.

Essentially a visitor can see the development of most home appliances from the 1850s to the 1950s. That collection of washing machines? One is dog powered. There are enough mousetraps in the collection to clean out an entire old schoolhouse, which is fortunate because the museum is in the old Murfreesboro High School. What else is on display? Phonographs, music boxes, butter churns. Jukeboxes, a pipe organ, and even a collection of church collection plates.

Considering the completeness of these items, that they are in amazing sets, curators from several other museums have wanted parts of the collection for their own displays. But Jefcoat wouldn't let his collection be split up. The Smithsonian's loss is Murfreesboro's gain.

94 Joe Sledge

Oddity ★★

World's largest collection of (fill in the blank)...

Difficulty ★★

The museum is only open on weekends, Saturdays from 11 am to 4 pm, and Sundays 2 to 5.

Pactolus Light

Pactolus & Stokes 35.68641° -77.24878°

This ghost story location is a little different from the Vander and Maco lights. The other lights involved workers on or near the trains, and there usually is a beheading. In this legend, it isn't the train's fault. Finally.

In the early 1900s, the actual date always seems to be a little vague, a young man went to the train depot near Pactolus to wait for his fiancée (sometimes it is his girlfriend and he is going to propose) to arrive on the train from Richmond. The train was running extremely late and he anxiously waited into the darkness. The young man had ridden his horse, a fine equine specimen, so his lady could ride back into town. Three men saw the man and his horse, and decided to bushwhack the poor guy so that they could ride the horse instead of walking. They attacked and killed the man and left his body hidden in the bushes. The horse was spooked during the assault, and ran away. It returned home riderless two days later, after which the family began searching for the man. They never found the body.

In later years, people began a seeing a ghost that walks the tracks as a ball of light. The light is figured to be the man, still trying to meet his fiancée so he can take her on her ride home.

The good news is this light seems to still be active. Other lights have disappeared when the tracks were pulled up, but even though the train tracks here are long gone, the Pactolus Light still makes appearances regularly. There are a large number of videos of the light appearing on the internet. Be warned that the light is rather spooky, and the reactions to it in the videos can be less than family friendly.

The Pactolus Light is similar to many other ghost lights in that there is a floating light on some abandoned train tracks, but what seems to make this different is both the number of claims seeing the light, as well as the sheer amount of hokum that has been created from stories about the light. To get the light to appear, some suggest blowing your car horn three times, or blinking your headlights. Other testimonials encourage the visitors to swear at the ghost to make it appear. The light may turn red. If the light changes to red, or immediately appears red, you must leave now, for you are in great danger! It also appears white, or bluish white as well. The light can be incredibly bright. It often chases people, putting them into states of unbridled fear as they run away. The light has been known to move at speeds estimated at up to sixty miles per hour. Which leads to the question, "Why bother running?"

Oddity ★★★★★

The Pactolus Light is extremely active, easily seen (if you believe in ghost tales), and massively spooky.

Difficulty ★★

It is down Carl Morris Road, a side road near Stokes. Driving on Carl Morris Rd., the light appears in a tree lined path that cuts through the road. Look for the tree lined path on the north side. While the pull off area is public, the property where the light actually occurs is on private land. If you want to walk up the abandoned rail line, get permission to go or you may face trespassing charges. Go at your own risk.

Central

112 Joe Sledge

Pioneer Giant Shriner (Going, going... gone?)

Roanoke Rapids   36.39294° -77.63141°

There are plenty of Muffler Men, Pioneer Giants, Giant Indians and their ilk throughout North Carolina. What makes this guy special? He's got a story behind his travels.

This giant started out as a jewelry salesman. Yes, this giant helped sell jewelry by towering over Elmo Garner's Jewelers and Home Improvement in Roanoke Rapids. After a rather oppressive sign ordinance was passed, and due to fears the giant may topple over into the nearby Exxon station, Elmo took the giant down around 1989 and gave it to the Shriners, to whom he was a member.

Now the giant proudly stands in front of the Shriners' building, in between Roanoke Rapids and Weldon, holding a Paul Bunyan-esque axe-like sign that says "Shriners help crippled children" on one side and "Tis Here" on the other. He sports an oil drum hat to represent the Shriner fez, complete with crescent moon and sword symbol.

Oddity ★★

The oil drum fez adds to the strangeness. At least, by the sign, you know he is a friendly giant.

Difficulty ★

By full sized or miniature car, anyone can drive right by this guy to see him. The Shriner giant stands in front of the Shriner's building on Aurelian Springs Road, south of Roanoke Rapids and Weldon.

UPDATE While there is no clear answer as to what has happened to him, it seems the Pioneer Giant Shriner has gone missing. It's hard to imagine a giant just disappearing, but that seems to be the case.

Second Hardee's (Going, going, ... GONE!)

Rocky Mount 35.94667° -77.79489°

Yes, the second Hardee's ever, the first real Hardee's building, is no longer. Hardee's founder, Wilbur Hardee, opened a burger stand in Greenville, near East Carolina College, now ECU, back in 1960. He sold hamburgers and shakes for 15 cents. Wilbur Hardee ended up selling his stake in the business to James Gardner and Carson Rawls. Over the years, Hardee had claimed that he lost his company in a poker game and that he had been inebriated at the time of making the agreement, but even he stated that ultimately he just made a poor business decision. Gardner and Rawls opened the first company burger restaurant in Rocky Mount, the first in the chain and first sit down restaurant, but technically the second Hardee's, in 1961.

The building fell into disrepair over the 10 years that it sat unused. The roof fell in and the windows were boarded up. There was some talk of refurbishing the building and possibly turning it into a museum for

Hardee's, but that never happened. The Hardee's company was taken over by the parent company of Carl's Junior, and the headquarters was moved from Rocky Mount to St. Louis.

The old Hardee's building finally was torn down in 2007. Currently the land is home to the Rocky Mount veteran's memorial, named for Jack Laughery, a Hardee's executive and veteran. Considering that Hardee's really got going when it built restaurants in Fayetteville, serving soldiers from Fort Bragg, the memorial is a good use of the land that started the chain.

Oddity ★

The land is now a noble piece of history. And you may still smell the "charco-broiled burgers."

Difficulty ★

The memorial is near the Imperial Centre and Children's Museum, with plenty of parking.

Mr. Hardee later started another hamburger chain, called Little Mint, which eventually had about 25 franchised locations in North and South Carolina. He called it that because Hardee thought he'd make a "little mint" with the business.

Concrete Dinosaur

Wilson 35.71691° -77.89916°

Oliver Nestus Freeman was a famous and prolific stonemason in Wilson County who had some pretty big name acquaintances, including Booker T. Washington and George Washington Carver. While it is not known if he was also friends with Fred Flintstone and Barney Rubble, Freeman did have a little fascination with dinosaurs.

Freeman was a student and teacher at the Tuskegee Normal School, later Tuskegee University, where he became friends with Washington and Carver. He became more than friends with another student, Willie Mae Hendley, whom he married. The couple moved to Wilson around 1910, where Freeman built a brick house and raised his family of four children.

In addition to doing the brickwork and masonry on some of Wilson's finest houses, Freeman made several concrete sculptures for many of Wilson's gardens. He also built his own brick house in 1910, which he converted into a stone bungalow in the 1920s. Freeman built a small round bungalow, now known as the Freeman Round House, for a rental unit when housing was needed for troops returning after World War II. He added stone and concrete sculptures to his property, including the now famous concrete dinosaur.

The Freeman Round House is now a local African-American museum. It features many of the tools and creations that Freeman would make, including sculptures made of concrete and seashells. The seven foot concrete dinosaur was donated to the museum by the Freeman family in 2003. It sits in front of the Round House, or at least as in front of it as can be, since the house is round.

Oddity ★★★

It looks a lot like Dino. The Flintstone's pet dinosaur, not the swanky singer.

Difficulty ★

There is no need to put your feet through your car's floorboard to stop here. A parking lot is next to the museum on Carroll Street. Check the hours to be sure to go when the museum is open.

Even though Oliver Nestus Freeman was probably a nice guy, people were afraid to go by his home. He kept three bears as pets.

Vollis Simpson's Whirligigs

Wilson 35.72249° -77.91301°

This may be the most legendary collection of roadside oddities in all of North Carolina. It would be hard to believe that there are people out there who haven't heard of Vollis Simpson's whirligigs. If they haven't, then they surely have heard of the legend of Acid Park.

Vollis Simpson was a creative outsider folk artist that was from Lucama, south of Wilson. During World War II, Simpson served on the Marianas islands. Without any of the usual comforts, stuck on the island, he decided to build a windmill that would turn a washing machine so they could clean their clothes in the tropical Pacific heat. He carried on his creative skills once the war was over. Returning to Lucama, Simpson began repairing farming equipment, and later moved houses. When his friends and business partners retired, rather than sit around watching TV,

Simpson started making his whirligigs, often out of the spare parts left over from his equipment repair days. These sometimes giant and sometimes diminutive moving art windmills sat up on poles near Simpson's workshop in Lucama. Using scraps from signs and reflectors, he made them spin, move, and swirl through the wind. The reflective surfaces created an amazing pattern of color, especially at night when a car's headlights were captured in the reflectors on the whirligigs.

Soon enough, Simpson's art took hold in museums. His whirligigs reside in, among other places, the High Museum of Art in Atlanta, the American Visionary Art Museum in Baltimore, and our own North Carolina Museum of Art. Private collectors and fans own pieces of his work. There are even some at the entrance of Fearrington Village, a housing development near Chapel Hill. His whirligigs were on display during the 1996 Olympics in Atlanta.

The bulk of his creative works were built on his own land, where they went up like tall colorful metal trees, swaying in the wind. The parts, little or big, all scrap metal, reflectors, old street signs, spun in harmony with the wind that would blow through the field and pond that was on Simpson's property. Some of the giant whirligigs were built into the pond. How he was able to construct them, then assemble them high over ground or water must have been an amazing sight. Some of the whirligigs are twenty feet tall or more, and sat on tall metal poles to reach up into the sky to catch the wind. They are just immense, and must be seen to be believed. Even then, to think that one man did all of them is hard to believe. They filled the little intersection near his workshop, and stuck out over even the towering trees of his land.

As Simpson aged, he was not been as able to continue to repair and maintain his windmills. Fortunately, the city of Wilson saw the value of this art and moved the whirligigs to a park in the town. The whirligigs were taken down and placed in storage, then restored and placed on display in the new Whirligig Park, an open air park with a grass pavillion for bands and outdoor events, including the Whirligig Festival, held in November.

Now, there is the legend of Acid Park. And it is just a legend,

completely untrue, which is important to remember because the truth of Vollis Simpson's life is a much better and happier story than the legend that came out of his work. Supposedly, Simpson, or usually an unnamed father, created all these sculptures out of grief. A young girl, usually said to be extremely high, was driving around a curve when she wrecked her car, wrapping it around a tree and killing the poor girl. In his grief, the father put up a myriad number of moving reflectors to catch the attention of anyone driving at night, so they would notice the curve and slow down. The story is totally untrue, just a legend created to scare high school kids. It has been refuted by many people, including Simpson himself, as well as his daughter, the two people who should know best.
Almost all the whirligigs have been relocated to Wilson, but there are still a few poles and one whirligig left at Vollis' old shop outside Lucama. See the original location at 35.658894° -78.054265°. It's the birthplace of the now official folk art of North Carolina.

Oddity ★★★★★

These are still some of the most amazing pieces of art on display in all of North Carolina. Now more easily accessible with them on display at Whirligig Park, you can get up close and see just how impressive the builds of these whirligigs are.

Difficulty ★

With the new park, many roads lead you into Wilson to see the whirligigs. There is plenty of parking all around the park, though it is closed off during their festival. They still look amazing at night, but be cautious in the dark.

Vollis Simpson died in 2013 at the ripe age of 94, after creating a massive number of whirligigs. He outlived his own ability to climb the poles to repair his art, but lived long enough to see them valued and preserved by a city and state that loved them.

Tee the Tastee-Freez Twin

Kenly 35.61301° -78.09044°

Somehow Tee got away from a Tastee-Freez and got a better job at Donnie's Corvette Specialists in Kenly. Well, which would you rather have, free soft-serve or a '68 Stingray? Tee is displayed on the corner of the garage, wired in to keep her from taking a tumble on any of the cars.

In the 1950s, Tastee-Freez created their mascots, Tee and Eff (get it? T for Tastee and F for Freez?) to advertise their soft serve ice cream. Tee was the female, with a strawberry swirl hairdo, while Eff, the male, had chocolate. The Tee here has her hair covered up by a top hat added later.

Tee and Eff always appeared naked in their advertising. With a big swirl of ice cream on their heads, you'd think they would want a sweater.

Oddity ★★★★

The big buggy eyes and the lolling tongue are strange enough, but having this odd naked thing waving to you from the roof sends this over the top.

Difficulty ★

Take the 'Vette in for a tune up, wave to Tee. Donnie's is on Highway 301, just northeast of Kenly.

UPDATE You wouldn't think that a place that restores Corvettes would just leave a naked Tee up there, would you? Tee got a new paint job with a tuxedo to match his top hat.

Country Doctor Museum

Bailey   35.77890° -78.12259°

The Country Doctor Museum in tiny Bailey starts out as a rather nice and simple collection of historic medical equipment and supplies. A closer look shows that there really is something more to this little museum.

Inside the museum are several unique, and rather odd, pieces of medical memorabilia. The tools of the medical trade of past centuries are sometimes strange enough to us of present day, but when the museum can say it has the actual tools that amputated General Stonewall Jackson's arm, well, that just increases the museum's credibility. Add a Civil War era operating table, an iron lung, and a full apothecary shop, and you have a great reason for stopping for a tour. The tour only takes about an hour, given by knowledgeable and pleasant docents who make the trip personal to you. The Country Doctor Museum is a sure cure for the tired traveler.

Oddity ★★

There are some really unique items for you to see. Definitely fill this prescription.

Difficulty ★

Bailey is a very cute little town just off Highway 264, near Wilson and Rocky Mount.

The Country Doctor Museum has one more very rare item. The museum is the possessor of one of three *Christ, the Apothecary of the Soul* paintings still in existence, showing Jesus in an apothecary dispensing Christian Virtues in glass jars.

ShadowHawk Western Town

Smithfield 35.42231° -78.24984°

There's a sheriff in town at Shadow Hawk. Not a new sheriff either. "Wild Bill" Drake is the sheriff, and founder, of ShadowHawk, a real live western town near Smithfield. Bill Drake is a semi-retired actor, originally from Kenly, who went out to Hollywood and got parts in various TV and movie westerns. He has graced the screen in cowboy cinema with parts in The Outlaw Josie Wales and Big Jake, as well as several episodes of Bonanza and Gunsmoke.

When Wild Bill came back to North Carolina, he brought the old west back with him. He began building Shadow Hawk with scraps of lumber, creating a Wells-Fargo bank. After that, he realized to have a true town, he needed a saloon, a jail, a chapel and a brothel. The town just kept growing. Wild Bill built everything himself without a level or straight edge. Far from being rickety, the town has a true old west feel of buildings put together by the pioneers who wanted something that would go up sturdy but fast.

Today, it sits as a real old west town. Nothing is just a front. Every building is being used for something. Neighbors and friends can come by to sit in the saloons, (yes, there's two of them,) and socialize. During the summer, it's open from noon til 10 pm during the week, and until 2 am on the weekends.

Wild Bill even continued his acting by shooting *Justice: The Colt .45 Way*. He plays a sheriff who shoots first and doesn't bother asking questions. His friends filled in as actors, and they, along with the videographer and editor all worked for free on weekends to create it. Additionally, the town has been used for commercials and movies.

Shadow Hawk is the real deal for cowboys and girls. Put on your vest and spurs, but leave the six-shooter at home. Sheriff Wild Bill don't like no trouble in his town.

Oddity ★★★

Don't be surprised when you hear the theme from *The Good, The Bad, and The Ugly* in your head. Or in your ears. Wild Bill plays real western music throughout the town.

Difficulty ★★

The entrance is at Wild Bill's house on a cul-de-sac in a neighborhood southeast of Smithfield. This is Wild Bill's backyard, not a business, and he sets the rules. Kids are welcome, and Bill doesn't allow any fighting, arguing, or cussing. But remember that there probably will be some drinking and smoking going on here. The town will be a little more hoppin' on weekends.

UPDATE Wild Bill Drake went to that great roundup in the sky in 2017, and there was some concern that ShadowHawk might suffer a similar demise. But it's back, with lots of help and support from fans and friends. They still have people showing up on weekends to see the town. And you can be sure Wild Bill is still there in spirit, keeping an eye out to keep the town safe from outlaws and rustlers.

Hills of Snow Snowball Stand

Smithfield 35.50775° -78.34020°

Hills of Snow in downtown Smithfield is a pretty clever looking building. Giant snowball buildings are pretty rare in general, and this may be the only one on the east coast. It has a few unique features not seen in any other snowball stands. The stand is a giant white cup, with a mound of blue shaved ice snow on top. Hills of Snow cleverly uses two straws in the big snow ice roof to form the Ls for the sign of its name. It is also one of the tallest snowball stands in the US.

Tommy Hill was the creator of Hills of Snow. After opening his snowball stand in a regular small building, he and his family built the current snowball stand in his backyard in nearby Selma back in 1984. The cup and ball were built separately and loaded onto a huge flatbed truck and taken to Smithfield, where it stands today.

The building, like all of the fantasy type buildings before it, was meant to draw attention. It was designed to drive home in the obvious and straightforward way exactly what you got from this place. But for Hills of Snow, there's a little more to it.

Most shaved ice stands use a grinder to chip off pieces of ice from a block. The ice comes off in small, rounded chunks. Then, a flavored syrup is poured over it, all sickly sweet and loaded with bright colors. No one really worries too much about what they get; it's cheap, cold, and icy on a hot day.

Sure, that sounds good, but Hills of Snow is different. And better. They keep their blade razor sharp, so the ice comes off like, well, snow. There are 101 different flavors, and countless combinations. They make their own syrups, with a pure cane sugar syrup from distilled water, not tap. In addition, Tommy Hill searched for only the best ingredients to make his flavorings, because he knew he was serving to people who would be coming back, day after hot day, and they deserved the best. Hills of Snow is still using his recipes today.

Now Tommy's daughter, Kristy Hill Hinnant, runs the place. Not much has changed with her running Hills of Snow, and not much needs to be changed. She added a few new flavors including some sugar free syrups, to help serve the needs and wants of her community.

So stand back and look over the menu for a while before ordering. There are just so many choices. Luckily, the Hills of Snow folks keep a list of some of the more popular flavors posted right up front. The best thing to get, though, is an add-on. Hills of Snow will pour sweetened condensed milk onto your favorite flavor, giving the ice a creamy, thick, luscious texture and flavor. Hills of Snow is a taste not to be missed.

Oddity ★★★

This blue dome roof snow-ball cup will keep you cool.

Difficulty ★

No one needs to climb onto the roof to slurp on the cool straws of Hills of Snow. It's right in the middle of Smithfield, with plenty of parking in the lot. Hills of Snow is closed in the winter. That's when they are up north getting more snow.

Kristy Hill Hinnant never got those snow cones at fairs or amusement parks. Her father wouldn't let her, because they wouldn't be nearly as good.

Vander Light

Between Vander and Steadman 35.02568° -78.76558°

Cumberland County has its own ghost light, and it's a pretty good one.

Sometime in the 1800s, on a dark, rainy night, Author Matthews, the ticket master for the train station near Vander, sat waiting for the evening train, which was running late. Concerned as to why it hadn't arrived yet, he grabbed his lantern and began walking down the tracks looking for a sign or hoping to hear the approaching train. In the dreary emptiness, the damp night soaked up all the sound, and no light from an engine broke the pitch black.

As Matthews arrived back at the depot, he heard a sound, a strange clicking noise, nearby. Turning back to look for the cause, he slipped on the stairs of the wet platform and fell on the rail, which knocked him unconscious across the train line.

The late running train finally approached the station. The engineer noticed the light from the lantern on the tracks, but did not notice

Matthews lying across the tracks until it was too late. Brakes squealed and sparks flew, but the train could not stop. Matthews was killed, beheaded, with his body torn to pieces. The only items still whole were his head and the still glowing lantern.

Soon after this incident, people started seeing a glowing light on the tracks near where Matthews met his end. Older legends tell of people seeing two lights, a smaller one that disappears while the other larger light remains. This was attributed to Matthews' cigarette being thrown to the ground as he looked for the cause of the rattle that ultimately sealed his fate. Contemporary reports do not mention two lights. Maybe Matthews gave up the habit. Smoking is bad for your health, after all.

The legend has some rather unique peculiarities. The Vander light is often seen from far away, coming toward the person watching. The light will get within a few feet of people, then vanish only to appear behind them, continuing on its way. The light is said to be extremely bright when up close.

One big note of warning. Trains have lights, too. They also have loud air horns and cause massive vibration and enough wind to knock you down if you are standing too close to the rails. And don't forget what happened to poor Author Matthews because he was *on* the tracks. If you see a train coming, get well out of the way. Better yet, just stay off the rails entirely.

Oddity ★★★

This is a pretty good ghost light in that people are still seeing it frequently. There are no other roads cutting across the tracks anywhere nearby, so it isn't headlights seen at a distance.

Difficulty ★★★

Since the light is only out at night, this is a dangerous ghost hunt. Parking near the railroad crossing on Old Vander Road is dangerous, and being out at night is dangerous. Then, you have to walk about a

quarter mile east in the dark, to the area near where the rail line splits, about .1 mile from the crossing, which, again, is dangerous. There is an empty sandy area just north of the railroad crossing, which may offer better parking.
But may be dangerous.
Seriously, scope this one out in the daytime, and be aware that the tracks are active. There is a path through the woods to the north of the tracks that will allow visitors to keep off the rails.

Arsenal "Ghost" Tower

Fayetteville 35.05466° -78.89429°

Part of the Fayetteville Museum and Civil War Park is the Arsenal Tower, a new artistic representation of one of the towers that were part of the original Fayetteville arsenal. The original arsenal was built from 1838 through 1853 as a response to difficulties in supplying the military during the War of 1812. Fayetteville built the arsenal in order to aid the federal military in having quicker access to an arms depot. The corners of the arsenal were four huge three story octagonal towers anchoring the walls. The towers were meant to be used as spotting towers and allowed for flanking fire, as well as office space on the inside.

During the Civil War, the arsenal served as a supply depot as well as for the manufacture of small arms, ammunition, and friction primers, along with other materials. One of the most famous weapons to come out of the arsenal was the Fayetteville Rifle, made with machinery captured at Harper's Ferry, VA. Today, a rare Fayetteville Rifle will sell for in excess of $25,000.

The arsenal stood until 1865, when Union General William Sherman marched into North Carolina, where he rolled through Fayetteville and overpowered the Confederate forces there. The Confederates evacuated, taking most of the equipment with them from the arsenal. Sherman didn't order the capture of the arsenal, but instead, following his usual path of destruction, ordered the building to be battered to the ground. For good measure, he had the rubble set on fire, effectively turning the arsenal to dust and ash.

The current tower is referred to as the ghost tower, an artist's representation of what the scale of one tower would have been when the arsenal stood. The tower is a white frame standing where the original northwest tower stood. There are also a few pieces of the original arsenal nearby in the park, as well as a series of markers for the original locations of parts of the arsenal.

Oddity ★★

It looks very nice lit up at night.

Difficulty ★

The ghost tower is part of the Museum of Cape Fear, which includes some remnants of the original arsenal. It is located on Arsenal Avenue. Note that the coordinates are for the actual Ghost Tower, but the museum, and its parking (and bathrooms) are on the other side of the highway, with a walking bridge that connects them. Park at 35.05467° -78.89297°.

Eiffel Tower

Fayetteville 35.03027° -78.93060°

The Fayetteville Eiffel Tower sits at the corner of the Bordeaux Center, a shopping center built in 1963. At about 80 feet tall, the tower is 1/12 the size of the original tower in France. It may not be as tall as the original, but there are many superlatives to the Bordeaux Center's tower over the French one.

Travel time for North Carolinians is much shorter, no airplane flights needed. If you get hungry there are plenty of restaurants nearby with food you can recognize. Really, what North Carolinian prefers pâté over pimento cheese?

There are Eiffel towers in Paris, Texas, Paris, Tennessee, and Paris, Michigan, but none are as tall as the 80 foot Bordeaux Center tower. The only replicas that can "tower" over this one are in large resort areas such as Paris Las Vegas or Paramount's Kings Dominion in Virginia.

Oddity

Perhaps if it was in LaFayetteville it would be more appropriate. Still, it's very nice looking and well kept.

144 Joe Sledge

Difficulty ★

It "towers" over the corner of Owens and Village drives. Parking is available in the shopping center lot behind the tower. You don't even need to speak French to find this, but if you want to, "Où est le Tour Eiffel?"

Former Grave of Robert E. Lee's Daughter

Near Warrenton 36.28241° -78.23646°

Annie Carter Lee, General Robert E. Lee's second daughter, along with her sister Agnes, left their home at Arlington, Virginia, due to the Union Army taking over the family's farm and land during the Civil War. They were sent to present day Warrenton, which at the time had mineral springs called Jones Springs, or White Sulphur Springs. Several months later, Annie contracted typhoid fever and died. She was only 23. Since her family was unable to return her remains to the family land at Arlington during the Civil War, the resort springs owner graciously offered to have her buried in the Jones family plot.

General Lee was never able to visit his daughter's grave during the war. He did visit her gravesite in 1870 before his death. Lee referred to her as his "little raspberry" due to a birthmark on her right cheek. Annie was considered quite gifted, but extremely shy due to a facial injury that left her disfigured and blind in her right eye.

In 1994, decedents of the Lee family petitioned to have Annie's remains moved to the Lee family crypt in Lexington, Va., at Washington and Lee University, where her father is buried. Annie rests there along with General Lee, Lee's wife, mother, and father, as well as other relatives. Lee's horse, Traveller, is buried in a plot outside.

While Annie Lee's remains no longer rest there, the cemetery still holds her grave marker, a tall obelisk made by a Confederate soldier after the Civil War. It sits in the corner of a small fenced off graveyard that contains members of the Jones family. The gravesite is not well maintained, with some vines and weeds growing around it.

Oddity

Even though Annie's remains have been moved, the monument marking Annie's grave is still there. It was built by a Confederate veteran.

Difficulty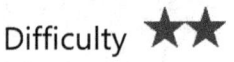

Annie Carter Lee's grave is marked on the main road by a roadside marker. The gravesite is off to the south on Annie Lee Rd. There is a short grassy pulloff to park a car, then a short walk to the gravesite. High grass, weeds, and bugs may greet you, but it seems that this site is open to public visits.

Soul City

Soul City 36.40837° -78.26514°

Soul City was a planned community dreamed up in the late 1960s by Floyd McKissick, a leader for CORE, the Congress of Racial Equality. He left CORE in 1968 to found Soul City, with backing from the federal government and funded by a HUD loan sponsored by an African–American owned development company. It was one of 13 new planned cities that began life during the Nixon administration, a shared utopia of a shining city on a hill. After 5 years, the town didn't show the growth that it dreamed, and by the end of the 1970s, the town was in foreclosure. The roads built to lead to the many houses planned for Soul City lead nowhere. Now, the town sits as much more of an empty shell than hoped, with a few hundred residents, a few businesses, and a sign that promised so much more.

> Imagine,
> A city without
> prejudice. A city
> without poverty. A
> city without slums.
> A city tailor-made for industry.
> A city with a booming
> economy.
> A brand new shining city.
> With open spaces. Trees and grass. Rolling hills. Soft winds.
> Fresh air. Clear skies. Where stars and moon are visible. Clean water.
> Lakes. Creeks. Ponds. Springtime weather. Hardly any snow.
> Yet distant mountains. Ample schools, hospitals, parking, recreation.
> Well built, stylish housing. A master plan. But not sterile and cold.
> For a city conceived with just an eye for bricks and mortar is a city
> without a soul. Call the bold alternative
> SOUL CITY.
> -promotional brochure from Soul City: The Bold Alternative

Oddity ★★

The town is so empty, and the sign seems to be crying.

Difficulty ★

There is little left to see. Most ghost towns still have buildings, but Soul City just has that totally unrealized feel.

Giant Concrete Legs

South Henderson   36.30075° -78.39951°

Ricky Pearce, sculptor, backhoe contractor, controversial artist.

After being inspired by seeing Marilyn Monroe in The Seven Year Itch, Pearce created these giant legs from concrete and lifted them into place with a crane. Painted in skin tone pink, they rise up 17 feet out of the trees on Pearce's land, with an entrance in wrought iron, spelling out 'Reminiscing'. Pearce even created high heels for the feet, but he couldn't get them to fit. They sit across the street on land that Pearce rents out.

Locals were divided on the legs when Pearce put them up. They definitely call attention to themselves. Some complained about the location of the sexy legs, saying they were poorly located because they were built between two churches. But couldn't that technically be said about anything?

Oddity ★★★★★

Odd, embarrassing, uncomfortable. As weird as this is, you kind of get the feeling that you want to take your pictures and get out of there before someone sees you.

(and probably, don't take your wife. – JS)

Difficulty ★

Don't hit it with your car! The legs are on the right side of Welcome Avenue as you drive east, off of US 1 in South Henderson, on the curve.

Gotno Farm (Going, going... saved!)

Raleigh 35.794993° -78.661057°

George Morris moved to North Carolina in the early 1920s to work as a plasterer for the Capital Construction Company during the construction of the Sir Walter Raleigh Hotel. He continued working until 1967, finally retiring from the plaster business and began farming on a small plot of land north of Raleigh. Plaster work was easier than farming for him, and the farm was not successful

Since he knew how to work with plaster and concrete, Morris began to make sculptures in his yard, mushrooms coming out of trees, animals like frogs and a giant concrete version of a toy dog, and some large planters. Morris became much more successful as a concrete artist than as a farmer. People came by to see his concrete environment for years. Morris even built a picnic area for groups who came by to see his work, and named the place, in a lighthearted nose thumbing at the more thriving growers around him, Gotno Farm.

On it he had many sculptures, most a mix of abstract strange shapes, some like coral coming up from the ground, while others were just unique shapes or large urns and planters. He even made a sign for the entrance. Plaster mushrooms sprouted from the ground and the sides of trees. Hidden in the woods, unseen to most passersby, was a lake with a large round shelter made of plaster and concrete for Morris and his family to use on nice days. He even added a replica of the Cape Hatteras Lighthouse.

His most famous sculpture was not one of his abstract works, but a much more recognizable and whimsical piece of art. It came out of a

rather disrespectful and mean comment from a kid. During a visit to his farm, a small boy was not impressed with the stuff he saw, and said so in no uncertain terms. Morris snatched a small toy from the boy, a little dog, and told them to come back in a week. When the family came back, there stood a giant replica of the dog, twelve feet tall, towering over everything else on the farm.

Time must move on, and George Morris passed away in the 1990s. His family rented out the house and property for a time. George had bought a new and rare building, a Lustron House, a prefabricated kit home meant to be cheaply assembled on site in order to provide good housing for soldiers returning to the US from Europe after World War II. The house is a rare one, as only thirty nine Lustron homes delivered to North Carolina before the business went bankrupt. When the property was sold for a new housing development, the Lustron and sculptures were at risk of going under the bulldozer's blade. So Preservation NC stepped in.

Preservation NC is referred to as "the animal shelter for old houses." They were able to remove both the Lustron House and the large dog. The Lustron will be preserved by new owners. The pup, now named George after his creator, will sit as a mascot for Preservation NC at their Raleigh offices. The dog is about all that is left of the history of Gotno Farm.

Oddity ★★

Most of the sculptures and the location they were in are gone now, so the setting doesn't have the same feel as when they were in the original place. The dog is still extremely impressive to see, and now visitors can get a little closer.

Difficulty ★

Gotno Farm is no more, but Preservation NC is rather easy to find, even in the tight neighborhoods of Raleigh. There's nothing left of Gotno Farm. It was at 35.83039° -78.57650° but there's just houses there now.

Morris made several Cape Hatteras lights. One is by the lake at the state fairgrounds.

Giant Ice Cream Bowl and Spoon

Raleigh 35.78612° -78.64716°

The Pine State Creamery is a building constructed in the 1920s for processing dairy products. By the 1980s, it along with most of the rest of this part of Glenwood Avenue sat empty and unused, but that would soon change. The Creamery would lead the charge back into the limelight for South Glenwood, with Sullivan's Steak House occupying the old processing part of the Creamery, serving up high end filets with a side of jazz and a martini or two to the legal and legislative crowd. The Creamery sports other restaurants, retail, office space, and loft apartments.

Of course, the best part of the Pine State Creamery is the big bowl and spoon on top of the building. On top of the deco tower sits an ice cream bowl on a saucer, with a spoon stuck straight down in the middle. While Pine State was well known for their home delivery of milk, one must guess that they probably had some pretty good ice cream to hold that spoon straight up.

Oddity ★

The Creamery was built in the moderne style during the 1920s. Moderne was renamed to the more recognized term Art Deco in the late 1960's when the style had a resurgence.

Difficulty ★

South Glenwood is a hip spot nowadays, so street parking, and restaurant tables, may fill up fast.

Giant Piano (Going, going... gone!)

Between Durham and Raleigh 35.94205° -78.82388°

This tall piano sat next to Piano & Organ Distributors in Durham. And probably has sat for some time unplayed. The giant piano sat, paint chipping, under their sign with some bushes growing up nearby. Hidden behind the trees and bushes, the piano began to rot and fall apart, so it was finally taken down and removed. The big old standup had to compete with a newer baby grand piano on a pole, wrapped in neon lights, no less. Unfortunately, neither the piano nor the business is there anymore. Some of these old subjects are just gone and lost to time, only to be remembered in a book.

Oddity ★★

It's too bad we will never hear what it sounded like.

Difficulty ★

Piano & Organ Distributors gone now, closed and empty. The old upright piano was torn down, along with the decorative piano key awning and the baby grand high on a pole.

Brontosaurus

Durham 36.02796° -78.90214°

The Durham Museum of Life and Science is crawling with dinosaurs. Or stomping with them, or whatever dinosaurs do. Did. Well, you get the idea. The museum has nine different dinosaurs on its trail in the museum grounds, including a large Alamosaurus, two Stygimoloch fighting, and a tiny Leptoceratops wandering the forest.

This isn't the first dinosaur trail, though.

Back in 1967, what started out as the Children's Museum built its first dinosaur trail, actually called the Prehistoric Trail, with eleven dinosaurs, a rhinoceros and a mammoth. Time and weather took a toll on the dinosaurs, like a sped up version of their time on Earth. Due to massive erosion in the early 80s from Hurricane Fran, the trail became unsafe for walking, and the dinosaurs fell into disrepair. Hurricane Hugo in 1989 caused immense flooding, which destroyed all the dinosaurs except the brontosaurus. What little was left of the original dinosaurs was collected and now is in storage at the museum. And what the weather couldn't do, vandals tried. In 2008, the brontosaurus lost his head to an ax. Luckily, it was found a few days later and the brontosaurus was repaired.

The brontosaurus is now protected behind a fence, to be seen, but not hunted. People who see the brontosaurus for the first time get to see the dinosaur looming in the forest as they walk down the trail. It truly is an amazing sight to see.

Oddity ★★★★

Seeing this thing is eerie! It just sort of appears through the trees as you get closer. If you don't know what to look for, it can be quite surprising.

Difficulty ★

You can park across the street at the nearby athletic fields, or at the museum if you want to see the new dinosaurs. Go in the summer when the leaves are full and green. The dinosaur looks cool as it slowly materializes out of the forest.

The brontosaurus dinosaur was never real. Its bones were discovered, without a head, in 1874 by paleontologist O.C. Marsh. In his haste to claim the beast, he put the head of a Camarasaurus on it. The body was actually that of an Apatosaurus.

Robot Tobacco Farmer

Durham   36.03590° -78.92127°

Duke Homestead is the home of Washington Duke, who grew the tobacco that would later allow his sons to found The American Tobacco Company. Among the things to see at Duke Homestead are the tobacco barn, factory, and the home Washington Duke lived in.

The best things to see, though, are in the museum. While the museum starts with the traditional historical views, models of the homestead, and information on tobacco, it goes into old cigarette ads, vending machines, and lots of memorabilia. But the very best thing visitors get to do is meet the scary robot farmer, who greets guests with a story about what it is like to grow and harvest tobacco.

He's a little larger than life, which probably is not that useful when picking tobacco The farmer gives a talk for about two and a half minutes, explaining the chores involved in harvesting tobacco in a nice, informative way. But there still is something slightly unsettling about the guy. Maybe it's the size, or the occasional arm movement for no apparent reason, or it could be how he doesn't seem to make eye contact with anyone, then all of a sudden he looks right at you, and you wonder if he can really see you. Is he going to ask you to help with the harvest, welcome you up on stage with that scary arm? When he's done talking, there is this slight feeling of guilty relief, just knowing he is done. The lights go down, the face stops moving, the eyes stop searching. Then he moves again, a shiver, a reset, this lifeless shift. And you back away quietly, not wanting to set him off again, children pressed behind your legs, slowly, slowly...

Oddity ★

He's no Cylon, but if his eyes turn red and he starts making that whrrr whrrr sound...

Difficulty ★

The entrance to the homestead is on Duke Homestead Road, naturally. The Duke Homestead is one of many nice places one can easily get to in Durham. It is closed on Sundays and Mondays.

In the old factory part of the tour there is a giant barrel that was used to store the tobacco for shipping to market in Durham. The barrels were so big that the easiest way to get them to town was to roll them. They beat down paths so well that roads were made from their passage. This maybe where the name "Tobacco Road" came from.

Giant Sundial

Chapel Hill 35.91443° -79.05095°

The University of North Carolina holds a special place in both in our home state and in the nation in that it is the first public institution of higher learning in the country. As an important science, astronomy was included in the first plan of education in 1792 at the founding of the university. By the 1820's UNC president Joseph Caldwell expanded the course of instruction by building the first observatory on a college campus, along with travelling to England to purchase telescopes and other equipment for instruction.

The study of astronomy grew intensely with the building of the Morehead Planetarium by John Morehead. Morehead built the planetarium after a comment by noted astronomer Harlow Shapley, director of the Harvard College Observatory. Shapley stated that North Carolinians were the most astronomically ignorant people in the country, because he never received any letters or questions from people in North Carolina about stars they saw in the night sky. Morehead said that if Shapley meant that North Carolinians are ignorant of astronomical matters, then he would fix that by building a planetarium for them.

In 1949, the Morehead Planetarium was opened after 17 months of construction. The planetarium was designed by the same architects who planned the Jefferson Memorial, and was the most expensive building ever built in North Carolina at the time. Morehead had to use his contacts in Sweden, where he formerly served as ambassador, in order to get a projector for the planetarium, as they were very difficult to obtain in the years after World War II. The planetarium was not only used as a science department for the university, it also trained astronauts in the Gemini and Apollo programs, including 11 out of 12 of the people who walked on the moon.

One of the most visible parts of the planetarium is the Morehead Sundial, designed by Joe Hakan, who was the chief engineer for UNC's buildings into the 1950s and 1960s. Hakan was tasked by John Morehead to build a sundial so accurate, he could rely on its accuracy to catch a train. In order to achieve this, Hakan stayed up nights at the spot of the sundial to determine the location of the North Star to correctly align the gnomon to true, and not magnetic, north.

The sundial is one of the largest in the world, at 35 feet in diameter and 113 feet around. The gnomon that casts the shadow used to determine the time is 24 feet long and 20 feet tall at the tip. On the base are inscribed two phrases, "Today is yesterday's tomorrow," and "It is always morning somewhere in the world." The sundial sits in front of the planetarium in a rose garden in the middle of the parking lot.

Oddity

No, it doesn't move. Only the shadow moves.

Difficulty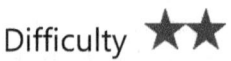

Chapel Hill is difficult for free parking. The lot for the planetarium is managed by UNC, which does not want to provide free parking for students driving to classes. You'll pay to park somewhere.

Dunce Cap on Wilson Library

Chapel Hill 35.91110° -79.05067°

A longstanding rumor around the campus of UNC-Chapel Hill has it that John Motley Morehead originally wanted to build a bell tower on top of the Wilson Library. Louis Round Wilson disagreed vehemently, not allowing Morehead to construct the tower there. In order to get revenge on Wilson, Morehead constructed his bell tower right behind the library, so that if a person stands in the middle of Polk Place quad, on the UNC seal in front of South Building, it looks like Wilson Library wears a dunce cap.

While much of this may be true, there really is no evidence that Morehead and Wilson had any disagreement. Neil Fulghum, the keeper of the NC collection gallery at Wilson Library stated in an article for The Daily Tar Heel that the Wilson library wasn't named for Wilson until 1956, 25 years after the construction of the bell tower. Of course, it could have been Wilson who said no to Morehead putting the bell tower on the library in the first place. And the library, even before it was named in his honor, was Wilson's idea throughout the 1920s.

Oddity ★

The only problem with seeing this is that UNC put a flagpole in the middle of the quad, messing up the angle a bit. It's a small price to pay for patriotism.

Difficulty

It has gotten harder to park on campus. Parking downtown and walking makes for a nice stroll and a good excuse to spend the day in Chapel Hill. Almost all public parking is metered now.

Gimghoul Castle

Chapel Hill 35.91196° -79.03610°

The best secret societies are the ones where legends so greatly overwhelm reality that what people think are going on significantly exceed the truth. Gimghoul Castle and the Order of Gimghoul does it like no other.

Gimghoul Castle is the site of a classic NC murder story. In 1831, Peter Dromgoole entered school at UNC. In 1833 he fell in love with a local girl named Fanny. Fanny was sufficiently charmed and returned Peter's affections. Peter and Fanny spent many days together in the nearby woods of Piney Prospect, next to the campus. Fanny had other suitors though, jealous of her love for Peter. One of them challenged Peter to a duel, and, after seconds were declared, the two met on Piney Prospect to carry out the act. The two stood, paced, turned and fired. Peter was shot and bled to death on the spot. Shocked by the realization of what they had done, the others quickly buried Peter and placed a boulder over his grave, the same boulder that Peter and Fanny spent the days sitting on in Piney Prospect. The other students made up a story that Peter, who was not successful as a student, had run away and joined the army.

Fanny couldn't believe that her love would run away without telling her, and she would go out day after day to Piney Prospect, longing for her beau, hoping he would return. She would sit on the same boulder that covered Peter's body, pining for her lost love. Some legends tell of her seeing Peter's ghost coming through the woods to her, but disappearing before being able to reach her. One way or another, Fanny was driven mad by the loss and died soon after.

The legend of Peter Dromgoole led some students to create the Order of Dromgoole in 1889, after hearing of the legend during a lesson on American politics. The name was quickly changed to the Order of Gimghoul, according to William W. Davies, one of the founders, "in accord with midnight and graves and weirdness." A development corporation was attempting to buy Piney Prospect, the area that held importance to the order, being the alleged location of Peter Dromgoole's death. In 1915, the order bought the area of Battle Park, in which Piney Prospect and the blood stained rock of Peter Dromgoole's grave sat, from the university. In 1926, a castle was completed for the order, with the bloody rock incorporated in the area. The castle was originally named Hippol Castle, but later became known as Gimghoul Castle.

Many secret societies are believed to have political or power issues. Unlike the rumors of Skull & Bones, Yale's secret society, the Order of Gimghoul has always professed to be only a social society, with no other ambitions. Again, the legend of the highly secretive and mysterious Order of the Gimghoul seems to outweigh the reality that it is just a very private, but social, club.

Not everything about the Order of the Gimghoul is secret. Many documents about the Order of Gimghoul exist in the Wilson Library on the UNC campus. One interesting find was a menu for a formal meal probably from 1892 that shows members enjoyed deviled crabs, claret wine, mustard pickles, roast turkey and cranberry sauce, biscuits, chicken salad, tutti frutti ice cream, fruit, and French coffee.

Gimghoul Castle and the bloody stone are at the end of a gravel and dirt road in the Battle Park historic subdivision. You can drive up the road to the castle, but the castle itself is off limits to everyone but members.

Oddity ★★★

Even though there are several "castles" in North Carolina, their commonness doesn't change the oddity. A ghost story always helps.

Difficulty ★★

Gimghoul Castle has such a legend to it that many think it is difficult to access. The castle is up a gravel road at the end of Gimghoul Road. Go when it's raining and play some scary music to enhance the effect. But don't go storming the castle. It's private property.

Clyde Jones Chainsaw Art

Bynum 35.77320° -79.13937°

There's a sign warning passersby of a "critter crossing," but you don't need to worry about these animals jumping out in front of you as you drive by. You will want to slow down. Then stop. And look, and look. A strange wooden menagerie gathers in the front yard of a little cabin near the end of the road in tiny Bynum. You have found Bynum's own celebrity folk artist, Clyde Jones.

Clyde does chainsaw art from tree stumps and branches. He creates wooden animals carved with a chainsaw, adorned with whatever he can find, and painted with every color he can imagine. All of them are cute, whimsical representations of animals, painted pink, white, yellow, whatever fits and sometimes doesn't.

Clyde got his start quite by accident. It was a serious accident, though. Clyde worked at the nearby mill until he was injured in a serious chainsaw accident that sent him home. While recuperating, he noticed a piece of wood that looked like the face of a piglet. He decided to put a body on the head, so he carved one up. It was so enjoyable to make the critter that Clyde just kept making them.

When driving into Bynum, you'll start to see the creatures appear by the side of the road. Alone or in pairs, they begin to perch by the houses of the residents of Bynum. They may distract you at first, with their smiling faces, as you turn onto Bynum Hill Road. But soon you will see the collection, including the tall giraffe wood sculpture at the head of a zoo of wooden critters looking like they are scampering across the yard.

When visiting Clyde's home you'll see many of his creatures, but you can't buy them. Not from him at least. Clyde has a famous story where dancer Mikhail Baryshnikov came to see his sculptures and Clyde refused to sell him one. Clyde doesn't make his art to sell. He makes them for himself, and others, to enjoy. Clyde does occasionally give them away though. His sculptures and paintings are sometimes donated and sold for charity at different events. They have also made the rounds to numerous museums throughout the US, as well as in collections abroad.

If you really want to get one, as well as see it made, you have one chance a year. In April, the Chatham County Arts Council throws ClydeFEST, with lots of kids' games, musicians, storytellers, magicians, many folk artists, and demonstrations of folk artwork. In the past, Clyde has ridden out there on his lawnmower. He found an easy way to get around the village and visit, so the lawnmower became his transportation of choice. He would sit out on his mower, greet kids, and give them temporary tattoos.

Clyde has gotten older, like all of us, and doesn't get out much now. In the past he would make a critter as a demonstration, then the mayor would auction it off. Clyde will probably not be making any more critters, but others hopefully will take up his mantle.

Bynum is close to Chapel Hill, so it makes a good diversion if you ever are nearby In addition to the critters, the local general store has been restored and they renamed it the Bynum Front Porch, where they do music and storytelling on the weekends.

Oddity ★★★★

Like Vollis Simpson's whirligigs, Clyde Jones' wood carved critters are an amazing and unique look at some great NC folk art.

Difficulty ★

If the Tar Heels aren't playing well, you can always head to Bynum instead. Bynum is off US 15. Turn on Bynum Road, then left onto Bynum Hill Road. You'll start seeing the critters before you even get to Clyde's house.

If you drive from Chapel Hill to Bynum on 15-501, you'll pass the housing development of Fearrington Village. At the entrance there are some of Vollis Simpson's whirligigs.

Occoneechee Raceway

Hillsborough 36.07008° -79.08566° (parking lot)

36.07406° -79.08156° (start finish line)

Occoneechee Raceway has been a staple for racing for decades, including years before NASCAR took over the track in 1948. In the late 1800s, General Julian S. Carr, the owner of Occoneechee farm, built a half mile red clay racetrack for racing his horses near a bend in the Eno River. The red clay was hard packed and sat over bedrock, making it not

easily farmed, but great for racing. In the 1940s, while flying over in his airplane, Bill France, Sr., saw the track and began the purchase of the land for his fledgling racing enterprise. By 1947, France, Sr. and his partners made the announcement to build a 1 mile track outside of Hillsborough.

Occoneechee Speedway, then called Orange Speedway, held racing events beginning in June of 1948, up to 1968. Occoneechee held its first Grand National race, then called Strictly Stock, on August 7, 1949. This was also only the third race held by the newly formed NASCAR racing organization. It was a 200 lap event in front of 17,500 fans, who got to see Bob Flock get his first victory in the series. And for the next twenty years, until 1968, the engines roared over the dirt and red clay of Orange County.

The last race at Occoneechee, on September 15, had a battle between two quintessential racers with Richard Petty on pole and David Pearson starting second. After contending for the lead for 120 of the 150 laps, Pearson's engine let go and Petty would go on to win. Orange Speedway would also see another end that year, as the legendary Curtis

Turner competed in his last race, finishing 14.

Occoneechee Raceway ultimately closed in 1968 when pressure from religious groups in Hillsborough finally shut the track down. It may have helped that Bill France Sr. had just built the massive Talladega Motor Speedway in Alabama the same year.

The track sat untended, but still on local maps, for almost the next 30 years, until in 1997 when the land was bought by Preservation North Carolina. The slight banking of the turns was still there, hidden by overgrowth and fast growing saplings. They cut down trees to expose the dirt track path, and cleaned away some underbrush.

Today, the original concrete stands still exist, along with a rebuilt snack bar, press box, and other structures on site. Future plans include clearing off the infield and continuing a classic car show and cool laps in historic stock cars from days past.

Oddity ★

This is the only racetrack still around from NASCAR's inaugural season. Take a walk in history.

Difficulty ★★

Finding the parking lot for the track is difficult if you don't know where to look. It's a short walk on a dirt path to the track, where you can circle the .9 mile raceway at your leisure.

Orange Speedway also hosted high school football games for schools in and around Hillsborough.

Large Rocking Chair and Adirondack

Hillsborough 36.02402° -79.14141°

A little ways off I-40 on Davis Road is Cooper-Payne's Tree Farm, which is pretty interesting in itself as they do landscaping that can include palm trees in your front yard. You just don't see that many palm trees in North Carolina. But what they have in *their* front yard is what is really amazing.

In the front of Cooper-Payne's farm is a very large rocking chair, and on the other side of the field is an impressive Adirondack, complete with a giant footstool.

Cooper-Payne used to have its location just off of I-40 near Hillsborough, and the chairs were easily visible from the interstate, but they were moved back to the farm itself when the business relocated, making the chairs a little harder to find.

North Carolina is home to quite a few large pieces of furniture, and there are several big chairs, Adirondacks and such, at several coastal spots, but few this big. These are big enough to make it difficult to climb into them. You have to see it to believe it. Hey, hop in one if you have the time. Just be sure to take your giant glass of lemonade with you.

Oddity

I mean it, these are big chairs. And there are two of them.

Difficulty ★

You can see them from the road. You used to see them from I-40, but they were moved, probably because people weren't watching where they were going and staring at the chairs. Watch where you're going! You'll miss the exit! It's on the south side of I-40, exit 261, then down a rather twisty Davis Road. The chairs are for sale, so they may not always be there.

Painted Barns

Cameron

35.32789° -79.27631° 8 buildings
35.31726° -79.28791° 6 buildings
35.33796° -79.31310° 2 buildings
35.31404° -79.26666° 1 building
35.31327° -79.24471° 1 building
35.33421° -79.27940° 1 building
35.33985° -79.32048° 1 building

In 1999, a group of 25 artists went to Cameron to paint several of the old tobacco barns and sheds that had sat abandoned or mostly unused on the outskirts of the little town. They call themselves the Barnstormers, a loose group of talented graphic artists that paint mostly in a street or graffiti style. The town welcomed the artists and allowed them to use the barns as canvases for the display of their art.

Led by David Ellis, a nearby Raleigh native, the group went down and painted 23 barns, as well as various other items in and around Cameron. In 2005, the group disassembled a barn, took it to Winston-Salem to the Southeastern Center for Contemporary Art, and each artist painted a design on the side of the barn. As soon as one finished, another would come and paint directly over the last piece of work. After all the painting was done, the barn was disassembled again, moved back to Cameron and painted over. Of course, after it was rebuilt, one of the artists came back and again painted on it. It now sits at a crossroads with seven other buildings and can be recognized because one of the artists in Winston-Salem opened the door and painted on the inside. That part of the older painting is still there.

Not all of the art is still visible. A few have been torn down since the first edition of this book, and others are being taken over by nature. Much of the paint is fading or chipping. But that is part of the Barnstormers style. The work is not permanent. It actually is meant to disappear, whether to fade away in the sun, chip and flake to the earth, or be covered with vines. And that makes the viewing of the works more impressive.

Each visitor gets to see the work in their own personal time. The artists go back every so often and paint new work over the old. It makes the place dynamic. As beautiful as a piece of art is, it is never irreplaceable. And you never know what could be there next year.

Oddity ★★★

Tiny Cameron is normally the home of some very nice old houses, a few great antique shops, and several farms. Not the place to expect to see some incredible public contemporary art.

Difficulty ★★

The barns are mostly right off the roads, but since many of these are no longer used, getting to them involves a little bushwhacking. Most places have either a place to pull off the side of the road, or a driveway of some kind. The locals are used to people visiting, so it is okay to do a little exploring, as long as you are respectful of the art and property. Some still store equipment. Wear heavy closed shoes or boots and long pants as the grass is long, and sometimes could poke you in your foot. And look out for biting ants. Stay off private property, as some of these barns are now in the back of people's yards.

Shangri-La

Prospect Hill 36.29971° -79.21490°

"When he started, he wasn't going to build much."

That's what Henry Warren's wife said about him building Shangri-La, a tiny town of stone, quartz, brick and cement built by the side of his home off of Highway 86 near Prospect Hill. In 1968, Warren, a retired tobacco farmer, saw a water wheel in an antique shop and decided he would build one like it on his property. He just kept building.

From 1968 until his passing at 1977, Warren built thirty structures for his miniature stone town. Shangri-La consists of buildings such as the Dew Drop Inn, White Rock Motel with a pool, a jail, doghouse, bank, town hall, silo, windmill, and an outhouse. Two unique buildings are the ABC store, and a replica of the Watergate building. The White Rock Hospital is still unfinished. It sits the way it was when Warren passed away in 1977.

Henry Warren loved having people stop to visit his little town. In the 1970s, Highway 86 was a well traveled road for tourists coming down to the beach from Virginia and northern states. Visitors could pull off the side of the road to take a break and wander around the village like benevolent giants.

These days fewer people visit Shangri-La than when Warren was alive. Highway 86 was rerouted a little so that drivers don't pass directly by Shangri-La and may not see it as easily to know to stop, which is too bad. The place still is in pretty good shape. It would take a lot of work to beat down the white quartz and concrete buildings. Sure there are some signs of age. Trees have grown into the windmill. Some of the figures have become chipped and weatherworn over the years. But like the real Shangri-La, it is still there. You just have to know how to find it.

Oddity

Feel like a giant from another time. Or Robert Conway.

Difficulty ★

Conway had to traverse mountains and suffer blizzards to get to his Shangri-La. This one is right off 86. The gas station that used to mark the area is gone, but you can look for the stone tower near the volunteer fire department as a landmark. Then turn onto the remnants of old 86.

Henry Warren paved his walkways with 11,000 arrowheads. He collected many of them from his land, but would also trade kids candy from the store where he worked if they brought arrowheads in for him.

Aunt Bee's House

Siler City 35.71651° -79.46600°

Frances Bavier, Aunt Bee from The Andy Griffith Show, retired to North Carolina in 1972 after having played Andy and Opie's long suffering aunt and housekeeper for ten years. On a visit to North Carolina for a Mayberry celebration she fell in love with its back roads and tall pines. She bought a 9000 square foot house in Siler City in 1972.

While sometimes perceived as a recluse, Bavier was social with friends in Siler City, though persistent fans often visited her unannounced at her home. Bavier was not very willing to open her home to unknown, unwelcomed, and unannounced guests. Who can really blame her?

Frances Bavier suffered from heart disease and cancer in her later life. She was admitted to Chatham Hospital the day before Thanksgiving in 1989. After spending two weeks in intensive care, she was released back home on December 4. She passed on two days later at her home from a heart attack.

The house is a rather impressive building. It is exceedingly large, at

9000 square feet. All the rooms have two doors, which allow anyone to walk through the rooms without having to turn around. Aunt Bee would have been diminutive in the house's 11 foot ceilings. There is ornate woodwork and hardwood flooring with crystal chandeliers above. It even has a recreation room in the basement. The house is now, and has been, a private residence. You can drive by to see the outside, but it is not open for visitors.

Oddity

Aunt Bee kept a clean house in Mayberry. Stories say that this house was less well cared for in her later days.

Difficulty

The house is all of 84 miles away from Mount Pilot. Maybe Barney can run you over in the squad car.

On one of Mt. Airy's Mayberry Days, one of Frances Bavier's checks was being auctioned off for autograph collectors. The description stated it came from her estate after her death, and it was "complete with cat fur."

Even though her character's full name was Beatrice, the shortened form of her name on the show was always spelled "Bee".

Aunt Bee died before Frances Bavier. When Andy Griffith and the rest of the cast made Return to Mayberry, a TV movie, in 1986, Andy tells the now grown Opie that he is going to visit Aunt Bee. He ends up at her grave.

Devil's Tramping Ground

Harper's Crossroads 35.58478° -79.48664°

What's for real about this place? There really is a spot in the woods near Harper's Crossroads, about 40 feet wide, with a circular path where nothing grows.

Of course, legend is so much better.

The Devil's Tramping Ground has been at least vaguely known of for about 300 years. There was a newspaper article written about it as early as the 1880s. Legend has it that the devil himself comes out at night and paces around the circle, plotting his nefarious deeds. He cannot stand anything to stay on his path, and any object left there will be moved out by the next morning. His hoofed feet, hot with brimstone, keep the ground sterile so that no plant grows there. No one can spend the night in the circle. They either leave in terror, or wake up to find themselves moved outside the grounds.

There doesn't seem to be any real explanation as to why nothing has grown in the circle. Studies show that the ground is sterile, and high in salt, which would inhibit growth, but there is no real cause for the salinity in that area. Various rumors run from a natural salt lick, the burial spot of Chief Croatan, a vortex of some sort, a UFO crop(less) circle, or perhaps something as mundane as a press used by mules walking endlessly in circles. But nothing is better for scaring easily influenced teenagers as the devil relentlessly pacing in circles night after night.

The tramping ground is starting to show its age now. While the path still is pretty much bare, the circle is getting smaller. The circle is less pronounced and it is more covered with organic matter, twigs, fallen leaves, rocks and pebbles. In the past the circle was much more bleached out and sandy, while now it looks a little more dirty and brown. The area gets trashed occasionally by people going out there at night having a fire in the center of the circle to see if anything happens. Unfortunately these visitors leave their trash from the night before. Maybe the devil doesn't mind beer bottles in his infernal path. There seems to be another unspoken legend in that anything taken from the circle will be cursed, so no one wants to clean up. That curse is more likely in the bottle, rather than the bottle itself.

Oddity

It is one of the oldest legends in North Carolina, and still unsolved.

Difficulty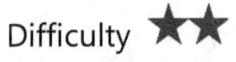

The road was even named after it. Look for the pull off down Devil's Tramping Ground Road.

First Miniature Golf Course in the US

Pinehurst 35.19812° -79.47618°

In 1916, Pinehurst resident James Barber had the first miniature golf course in America designed for his home. After completion, Barber, to his designer, Edward H. Wiswell, is said to have declared, "This'll do." Thus was created the first mini golf course, Thistle Dhu.

Thistle Dhu was a little different from future golf courses, in that it used compacted sand instead of grass, but there were fountains, statuary, and paths from hole to hole. Thistle Dhu actually set the stage for modern mini golf courses. There had been other non-traditional courses before Thistle Dhu, but they were more miniature versions of regular golf. The courses consisted of longer, 50 to 100 yard holes, using a short driver and a putter. Thistle Dhu was compact, classical in its style. The player only needed to use a putter, though a few holes could be played with a 9-iron. Miniature golf courses of today are made more inthe style of Thistle Dhu than the old, undulating courses of St. Andrews.

James Barber donated his land to the local Catholic church in the 1920s, but this house is now owned privately. Happily, the house was sold since first writing about it, and has been massively refurbished. The original front entrance has been restored and the entire property cleaned up. It can be seen from the street but is not currently open for visitors.

Oddity ★★

Where else but Pinehurst would you find the first mini golf course?

Difficulty ★

It is easy to pass by Thistle Dhu, but the remnants of the miniature golf course, if any, are hidden in the yard. It is a beautiful house, but there's nothing much more to see right now.

The very first miniature golf course, created at St. Andrews in Scotland, was built for ladies, because ladies were not allowed to swing clubs over their shoulder.

To honor the original mini golf putting holes of Thistle Dhu, Pinehurst Resort built their own Thistle Dhu, a practice putting green set of holes at their two famous courses.

World's Largest Strawberry

Ellerbe 35.04137° -79.76666°

Strawberry ice cream, for those who ever worked at an ice cream shop, is the bane of the scooper. It is always difficult to scoop, hard, brittle, with big chunks of strawberries that make the scooper have to slice through frozen fruit.

But, oh, is it soooo good.

The Berry Patch started as a small farm back in 1995, by Lee Berry (no, he doesn't grow straw). His wife, Amy, came up with the idea of building a stand shaped like a strawberry since they were growing strawberries on their farm. The stand sells produce, cider, jams, and their delicious homemade ice cream.

They make all their ice cream themselves, and it is creamy, fruit filled, and luscious. The Berry Patch makes 19 different kinds of ice cream, including, in addition to the usual flavors, peanut butter, banana, orange pineapple, and of course, strawberry. The Berry Patch moved from its old location in 2012 to near the junction of Highway 220 and the 73/74 bypass just south of Ellerbe. It is open from April to mid November, but you can pass by the stand on Cargo Road/McIntyre Road anytime.

Oddity

You can eat the ice cream, but don't eat the building.

Difficulty ★

The Berry Patch is just off the interstate at exit 8, just south of Ellerbe. It is visible from the highway going north. While The Berry Patch lists its address as Cargo Road, maps show the road as McIntyre Road as well. Either way, it is still pretty easy to locate. This is one berry patch where you don't have to stoop to find the strawberry.

Mystery On-Ramp

Mayodan 36.41781° -79.93721°

There's a mystery on-ramp in North Carolina. The northbound on-ramp to US 220 N from 311 where it crosses 135 by the Wal-Mart defies gravity. Going only about a tenth of a mile down and stopping, a car will then slowly back up the hill. While this can be dangerous to try in the road, luckily enough people have done this to smooth out the side of the on-ramp so cars can pull over to the side of the road. This may be a fun little diversion for anyone visiting nearby Mayodan or Madison, or maybe on the way up to Martinsville, Va. Just remember the danger involved in doing this. The car really will roll uphill backwards, and pretty fast. And other cars will be coming down (up?) the on-ramp, pretty fast. And you won't be looking out the back window while you face forward. If you actually want to try this, keep your foot on the brake, and keep the engine running. But it might be better just not to try.

Oddity ★★★★

Sitting in a stopped car and then having it start to move, uphill, on its own, is just spooky. Keep your foot on that brake!

Difficulty ★★

It is pretty easy to find, but finding the sweet spot may be difficult. It seems like you can really get rolling up the hill from pretty far down. But with all the traffic, this just probably makes it a don't try. And you don't want to roll into the ditch on the side either.

World's Largest Chest of Drawers

High Point 35.96354° -80.00830°

At 38 feet tall, High Point's Bureau of Information has stood as the largest chest for drawers since 1926. It was built to honor High Point as the furniture capital of the world and also serve as the town's Chamber of Commerce. The building originally was a two story dresser. In 1996, the building was remodeled to the current three story design seen today. The socks were added to honor the hosiery industry of the area. The original Goddard- Townsend chest that was the model for the building sits inside the lobby.

Jamestown 35.97013° -79.92520°

The Jamestown chest is part of Furnitureland, a huge furniture complex that uses its highboy chest to highlight that it is the largest furniture store in the world, with over a million square feet of showroom space. The highboy is 85 feet tall, and is attached to the front of the main building at Furnitureland.

So, what is the difference? Since the Furnitureland piece is twice as tall, how come it isn't the largest chest of drawers in the world, and High Point's bureau sent to the attic of giant furniture in obscurity? Well, it's a question of definitions. The High Point chest of drawers is just that, three long drawers and two short drawers. A highboy is different in that it usually consists of a chest of drawers on the bottom and some long drawers on the top, with some double and triple drawers as well. Highboys were popular in the 18th century, when the drawers on the top were so high up that at the time, people had to use bed steps to reach them. Bed steps were little steps used to climb into tall beds with big mattresses. When tall beds became less popular, there was no need for the bed steps.

So the highboy became a sort of collateral damage, disappearing as the bed steps disappeared.

Oddity ★★★

You'll need bed steps the size of Fayetteville's Eiffel Tower to reach the top drawers at the highboy in Jamestown. The socks in High Point may fit on the feet of Ricky Pearce's concrete legs.

Difficulty ★

The only way to make these things hard to find is if High Point starts making all its buildings into furniture. High Point's chest of drawers is on North Hamilton Street, which runs parallel to Main Street. Turn off Main onto East Westwood Avenue to drive right up to it. There is plenty of parking around the back. The Furnitureland highboy can be seen from Highway 70. Park in the Furnitureland lot.

Lydia's Ghost

Jamestown 35.99687° -79.92577°

This is one of the biggest, most classic ghost stories in North Carolina. Lydia is the ghost of a young woman who was killed in an automobile accident while coming back from a dance late at night.

The legend of Lydia's ghost begins with Lydia and her date driving home to High Point on a rainy dark night from a dance in Raleigh. Her date, driving the car, was speeding down the dark twisted road of Highway 70.

Approaching the tunnel in Jamestown where the train tracks go over the highway, the car goes into a skid, crashes, and kills the driver. Lydia, stunned and bloodied, climbs from the car and tries to flag down any approaching motorist for help, but no one wants to stop on this rainy night for a drenched and bedraggled person in stained and ragged clothes. Lydia succumbs to her injuries on that lonely highway in the cold night and dies.

In the years afterwards, a young girl in a fancy evening dress would often appear at the tunnel, attempting to flag down a driver for a ride. After getting a ride from a passing kind young man, she tells her story of being at a dance, having a fight with her date, and getting kicked out of the car. Her name, she says, is Lydia, and all she wants is to go home. She gives the driver an address to a house in High Point, but says little else. She doesn't respond to any questions, so the driver finally gives in and drives her home in silence.

Once there, the gallant driver gets out and goes around to open the passenger door. When going around to open her door, he finds she is gone, no longer in the seat. Figuring she must have jumped out as soon as he did and ran to the house, he goes up to the door and knocks, wanting to make sure the girl got in safely.

It's late at night, and it takes several knocks to get someone to come to the door. Finally, a tired older woman answers. The driver asks about the girl, did she get inside okay, is she alright? The woman at the door explains that the girl is her daughter. Yes, her name was Lydia, and she passed away in a car wreck on the same stretch of road where the driver picked her up earlier that night. It was Lydia's ghost that waved him down. After all these years, Lydia is still just trying to get home.

There are several twists that often attach themselves to this story. Sometimes Lydia leaves an item in the young man's car. One story tells of how the driver gives the poor shivering girl his sweater, and, when told that Lydia actually is dead, visits her grave the next day only to find his sweater neatly folded next to her headstone. Sometimes Lydia is kicked out of her date's car, and is hit by another on the dark curvy road in the middle of the night. But the gist of the story is always there. The funny thing is how, no matter how many years later, the driver always meets her mother at the door. Does that woman ever age?!

Oddity ★★★

Yeah, it's just a tunnel, but it's a haunted tunnel!

Difficulty ★★

Since the state redid the tunnel, it is easier to spot. But parking is still difficult. The nearby electrical property is covered with rocks and high grass, but there is a small gravel driveway to a fenced off road. Parking is available on the side street. There also is an access road right next to the train tracks that leads to the tunnel. Be very careful and stay off the train tracks! They are still used regularly.

Lydia's ghost does not appear at the old tunnel, now more of a drainage tunnel, since the road had been moved about 100 feet over. She now appears near the new underpass, the much wider bridge for the train track. It seems that Lydia is clever enough to move over to where she is more likely to hitch a ride.

In the past, mischievous boys would hang white dresses or slips from the railroad bridge to scare drivers on dark nights.

Big Red Bicycle

High Point 35.98130° -80.02201°

Yes, that is a giant red bicycle on the roof of Bicycle Toy and Hobby in High Point. The bike shop was started by Jesse Jennings in 1927. The shop sold other items, as shown by the company name, but began focusing on bicycles after the store was moved in the 1940s. Jesse's son Danny took over the business and moved the store to the current location in 1986. It probably was fitting to move to that building since it had a giant bicycle on top! The bicycle was actually built by the folks at Bicycle Toy and Hobby.

Bicycle Toy and Hobby is now much more of a bicycle than a toy shop, but it does hold something inside that you won't see from the street. Danny Jennings has one of the largest collections of bicycles in NC. It is full of racing bikes from the 80's, as well as old Schwinns, pedal cars, and beautiful banana seat Krates. The collection can be arranged to be seen, but those bikes aren't for sale. They have plenty that are, though, and Bicycle Toy and Hobby can definitely find a bike that is perfect for you.

Oddity ★★★

The bike is not really a specific model, but is based on a Schwinn racing bike.

Difficulty ★

Easy to find, but difficult to see. Parking in the shop's parking lot will leave your view blocked by the tall building. The better view would be across the street. Be careful, Main Street is a busy five lane road. Watch where you are going when you pull out onto the road.

Duncan Phyfe Chair

Thomasville 35.88290° -80.08198°

World's largest chair? World's largest *chairs*? Is Thomasville home of the world's largest Duncan Phyfe chair?

The town of Thomasville has had two giant chairs grace their town center over the years. Thomasville actually had their first big chair built in 1922. It was a real chair made of enough lumber to make 100 regular size chairs. The seat was covered in leather. The Thomasville Chair Company built the chair as a tribute to the town being known as "The Chair Town." The original chair stood in about the same spot as the one today, in the middle of downtown Thomasville across from the train depot. At 13 and a half feet tall, it took 3 men working ten hours a day an entire week to build.

The first chair stood for nearly 15 years, but weather and the elements took their toll on the wooden frame and leather seat. Still, that's pretty good for a chair left out in the rain and snow for 15 years. The town almost immediately began plans for another chair and for several years the idea was tossed about and planned. It wasn't until after World War II, in 1948 actually, that the new chair would finally be built. This time the chair would last. The Thomasville Chamber of Commerce asked sculptor James Buford Harvey to build the giant chair out of concrete. Harvey, who made a concrete lion sculpture near the current chair, created a concrete over steel frame chair. The design was created with the help of Thomasville Chair Company's Thomas Johnson, their dean of designers. He created the design for a Duncan Phyfe chair, and Salem Steel Co. built the steel frame. Harvey labored over the frame, adding concrete in small amounts until the chair was completed. The chair was painted to resemble wood and cloth, and the Chamber provided the pedestal base upon which the chair rests.

The total height of the display, from the base to top is 30 feet, with the chair 18 feet tall and a seat 10 ½ feet across. There is no normal access to the chair, but that hasn't stopped people from sitting on the chair. Governors, mayors, and beauty queens have graced the chair over the years. They just needed a ladder to get in it.

Oddity ★★

If Thomasville wanted to make this even more odd, they could tuck a giant remote control into the back of the seat.

Difficulty ★

There is plenty of parking along Thomasville's main roads, so don't stop in the street by the chair. It's right next to the railroad tracks, and no one wants to get caught on those things.

The chair's most famous "sitter" may be when then vice- presidential candidate Lyndon Johnson stopped by for a whistle stop visit.

Körner's Folly

Kernersville 36.11522° -80.07868°

"That will surely be Jule Körner's folly."

Don't be fooled. In this case, folly doesn't mean what you think it means. This house is no act of foolishness. In the 19th to 20th centuries, folly for architecture meant a building that was more for decorative reasons than for practical purposes. Körner's Folly was not built as a fool's errand. It merely is strange.

The building was started in 1878 by Jule Körner as a temporary bachelor pad and an office for his growing interior design business. During the construction, a cousin uttered the illustrious phrase above. Körner liked the phrase so much, it ultimately became the name for the house, and ended up set in tile at the foot of the front door.

Körner finished the original house in 1880, but continued to adjust and add to the property for years. Since the house was meant as a means to showcase Körner's interior design ability, all the rooms are different, with diverse designs and sizes throughout the house. There are twenty-two rooms in the house. The house has three floors, but the way the rooms are built mean they sit at seven different levels. The ceiling height throughout the house ranges from 6 feet to 25 feet. One of the most unique aspects of the house is that none of the doorways are the same size. Körner utilized a complex system of windows and trap doors to create airflow throughout the house way before air conditioning. If that wasn't enough, fifteen fireplaces kept the house warm on cold days.

The home went through several major changes throughout Körner's life. In 1886 Körner married Polly Alice Mastern. Since Körner no longer needed the place as a bachelor pad, she did some serious remodeling. She had the stables next to the house closed in and moved the horses across the street, turning the original stables into a library and sewing room. The original plan for several other buildings never materialized. Too bad, because Körner planned to have underground tunnels so that people could move from house to house without getting wet on rainy days.

Körner passed away in 1924, and the house stayed in the family, being used occasionally up through World War II. In 1970, with the house in disrepair and facing the wrecking ball, it was bought by a local group of twenty-six people with the intent to save the house and restore it to its former beauty. The work is still in progress, but the house is open for tours. Guests get to see interior design, the unique features, and the restoration process. The decorations on the inside defy description, and must be seen to be believed.

Oddity ★★

The inside of Körner's Folly is a mixture of the strange and the magnificent

Difficulty ★

Körner's Folly is on South Main Street in Kernersville. Parking is next door. Your only difficulty will be in not wanting to leave.

Körner's Folly was unique and ahead of its time in several ways. In modern homes many people have spent considerable money to create home theaters, areas with large televisions and theater seating. Jule Körner had a home theater in his attic in the 1896. The Little Theater held puppet shows and plays. Out front of the door was a cauldron with the words Witches Corner in tiles. This was a spot where guests would throw a coin into the pot. Any witch would be distracted by the sound and shine, then wouldn't be able to get into the house when the guests entered.

Kernersville was originally named Dobson's Crossroads. George Washington ate breakfast at Dobson's tavern in 1791.

Shell Gas Station

Winston Salem 36.06766° -80.21411°

This Shell gas station was one of eight shell shaped gas station buildings built in the fantasy style in the 1930s. R.H. Burton, a local Shell dealer, built them to attract customers. They would know what gas they were getting even if they didn't see any sign along with these buildings. The shell of the Shell station was made of bent wood and wire, with concrete stucco applied to make the distinctive ribs. The building was then painted Shell yellow.

The other buildings are now gone, lost to time, shut down in the 1950s. All the others were torn down at one time or another, but this one still stands. For a while it was a lawn mower repair business. J. Don Watson rented the building in 1970, and bought it in 1980. By then the wooden frame was slowly coming apart. That's when Preservation North Carolina got involved. Restorer John Larson helped to tie the building back together and restore the Shell station to its former glory. Today it stands as not only a beautiful reminder of buildings long gone, but it also is a regional office for the PNC. Inside are a few remnants from the station's past, including pieces of the old Shell visible gasoline pumps.

The Shell station is fully restored, but does not sell gas anymore. The history is free.

Oddity ★★★

The Shell station is one of a kind, and the last of its kind.

Difficulty ★

Fill up your tank with architectural history at the corner of Sprague and Peachtree Streets.

This was the first individual gas station to be placed on the national register of historic places.

Big Coffee Pot

Winston-Salem 36.09083° -80.24284°

The symbol of the united towns of Salem and Winston has a little showiness of pride in its upturned spout. It has long been recognized that the Old Salem coffee pot, not the brightleaf, is the image of Winston-Salem. And what could be better than this image of community, of everyone sitting down to share a cup of coffee?

The coffee pot has an enormous heritage, almost as big as the pot itself. It was created by tinsmiths Julius and Samuel Mickey in 1858. A few years earlier, the Mickey brothers had opened a grocery store on the corner of Main and Belews Creek Streets in Salem. Because the property had an empty lot, the brothers Mickey added a tinsmith shop next door. Fortunately, they were skilled tinsmiths, and business was good. Tin is a soft, easily malleable metal that could be made into many useful items, from lanterns and plates to bedwarmers and buckets. It was cheaper than products made of iron, and it looked nice and shiny. Soon, the tinsmith business was doing better than the grocery store.

Unfortunately for the Mickeys, they had competition. Down the street was another tinsmith, and whenever someone came looking for Mickeys' tin shop, he would steal the business away from Julius and Samuel. So they did what any good businessmen would. They advertised.

In 1858, the brothers built the big tin coffee pot, and stuck it on a pole next to their shop. The pot is said to be big enough to hold 740 gallons of coffee. Sometimes the amount is said to be 740 cups instead. The pot is 64 inches across at the bottom, and 7 feet, 3 inches tall. There have been several other measurements given for the coffee pot in the past. Some may have included the pole as the base, but this thing is a big pot of coffee, so it definitely holds a lot.

The coffee pot was mounted on a pole at the corner of Mickeys' lot back in 1858. Actually, the pole sat at the corner, so the giant base hung out over the road, creating quite a hazard for passing carriages. One such speeding passerby knocked the coffee pot so hard it came off its pole and careened across the road, nearly bowling over, or perhaps boiling over, a woman and child. The town leaders demanded that the coffee pot must go. It was too much of a danger, as well as being illegal to use as an advertising sign. The pot had become a rather endearing symbol for the united towns of Winston-

Salem, but it had also become a bit of a nuisance to travel.

After sitting in the back of the store for about four years, local leader Henry Fries championed the coffee pot and its return to prominence. Henry Fries was a person used to getting things done, and getting his way. In the late 1800s, Fries completed a rail line over the mountains to connect Winston-Salem with Roanoke. He later helped create a line to Wadesboro, making Winston-Salem a highly viable and connected city. Saving a coffee pot was easy.

The town officials relented, and the coffee pot was reinstated, albeit a little bit farther back from the road this time.

The coffee pot got in the way of traffic one more time, and in a big way. Big, as in Interstate 40. The new interstate would run right through the post of the coffee pot, and the engineers of I-40 were not about to move the road for a coffee pot. So the pot was moved again, to a grassy spot at the top of Main Street in Old Salem, where it still sits, ready to pour its 740 cups to open the eyes of every visitor and resident alike to Winston-Salem. Or is that 740 gallons?

Oddity ★★

Starbucks has nothing on those Moravians when it comes to coffee. Cookies, either.

Difficulty ★

Even bleary eyed and tired, anyone can find the big tin coffee pot at the top of Old Salem.

Legends about the coffee pot are innumerable. They include...
A civil war soldier, usually a Yankee, hid in the coffee pot by crawling in the trap door at the base.
Also, when Union General Stoneman and his troops passed through, they were served coffee from the pot.
There are various legends of serving coffee to the Moravians during Easter and the Love Feast.
One tale mentions a boy climbing into the pot to start a fire in order to boil water so that steam would come out the spout.

The coffee pot historically marked the border between Salem and Winston. Up through the 1940s, Bishop Howard Rondthaler, dean of Salem College, used the coffee pot to delineate the line where his students could go without signing out. Winston, north of Salem, was considered an unsafe place for the virtue of his female students.

Based on the measurements given by the Wachovia Historical Society, the coffee pot is 64 inches at its base and 7 feet, 3 inches tall. Which would mean it would contain about 403 gallons, or 6448 cups of coffee

Fisk Tire Boy (Going, Going,... Gone!)

Rural Hall 36.21249° -80.28387°

The Fisk Tire Boy sits atop an old disused gas station in Rural Hall. The Fisk Tire Boy began his life in the early 1920s as an ad with the slogan, "Time to retire." The play on words showed a small boy yawning with a candle in one hand and a Fisk tire in his other. The plaster tire boys were created in the 1960s for use outside Fisk and Uniroyal sellers. There was also a matching smaller statue on the inside of most shops. This tire boy is missing most of his paint, his candle, and his tire, but is in good shape otherwise. He still seems pretty sleepy.

Oddity

This is great retro kitsch at its best.

Difficulty

The Fisk Tire Boy sits on the roof of an abandoned gas station just south of Rural Hall on Highway 66/University Parkway. There are still remnants of the station's pumps and sign, but this place can easily be missed. On the opposite side of the road and just north of the station is a large RV sales lot. Go see him now. He's getting tired of waiting.

218 Joe Sledge

UPDATE Now, not only are the Coca-Cola signs gone, but so is the Fisk tire boy. It was taken down a while ago. All that is left is a mildly interesting run down gas station, with the concrete stands for the pumps and a light hanging forlornly over an otherwise empty lot.

Metalmorphosis

Charlotte 35.15079° -80.94802°

It's a giant silver head. It comes apart. It spins around. It slowly shakes. It turns.

It spits water.

This is David Černý's Metalmorphosis. It is a giant spinning head that comes apart into 7 sections and rotates each section in the opposite direction of the one above or below it. Then it will reform, and slowly shake its head back and forth. Then, for no apparent reason, it just turns the other way. Time it right and it will seem like the head is looking at you. Or totally freaking out.

This artwork comes from Czech sculptor David Černý, who got his start by painting a Soviet tank pink. Which would be kind of odd in and of itself, but what makes it even better was that the tank was sitting on top of a big stone pedestal in the middle of Prague, in 1991. See, the Soviets were still sort of in control then.

Since then Černý has done other works, including rather large babies climbing up a TV tower in Prague, a sculpture of a man hanging by one hand on a pole high up on a building, and Charlotte's own Metalmorphosis. Let's hope he keeps up the good work.

Oddity

Yes, it really does spit water.

Difficulty ★

Park in the side parking lot and walk right up. Some people park on the street when it's not business hours. Also, this thing looks incredibly creepy at night.

It is rumored that the artist has a remote control to the Metalmorphosis sculpture back in Prague.

Love Valley Western Town (Going, going...?)

Love Valley 35.98736° -80.98841°

How did Love Valley get its name? There turns out to be a pretty simple reason for this affectionate moniker. When founding the town, Andy Barker said that he loved people, and he wanted to call it "Valley of Love," but that was too long, so it became Love Valley.

Andy Barker created this town because he always wanted to be a cowboy. He was, however, a very successful contractor in Charlotte. So in 1954, when he was 29, he combined the two careers by purchasing the land that would become Love Valley, a real live western town. This is no rawhide staged fake storefront Wild West façade, but the real deal. The road is dust and clay, and the only way into town is on foot or horseback, which has become the popular mode of travel there.

But this is not an "old" west town. Love Valley has gift shops and restaurants, tack for your horses, cabins for rent, and a hardware store which was owned by Andy, of course. Love Valley has electrical power, ice cold sodas, and hot food.

Love Valley also had a bit of celebrity for a while. What western town would be complete without a blacksmith? And not just any blacksmith, but the strongest man in the world, Joe Ponder. Joe Ponder was known for feats of strength using his jaws and teeth. Joe had no problem lifting giant pumpkins, horses or beautiful women, all with his teeth. Joe pulled trains, trucks, and even a steamboat!

Joe Ponder and Andy Barker are no longer with us, but you can visit Love Valley in Iredell County whenever you pass by Statesville or are wine tasting in Yadkin County.

UPDATE With issues with plumbing and water supplies, Love Valley has had problems with staying open, in the past. The good news is that they may have solved many of these problems. The town stores generally are only open on weekends, but they still have camping, rodeos, and other events. You may want to check their online schedule before planning a visit.

Oddity ★★★★

A western town, a *real* western town? Love Valley is also known as the only place east of the Mississippi to have had a marshal instead of a sheriff.

Difficulty ★

There's parking right next to the sign. You don't need a horse to get to this town, but it helps.

Love Valley had a jail, but when Andy built it, the state wouldn't let him use it, because it didn't meet correct standards for a jail. Barney Fife would have had a fit.

Mountains

Tom Dula's Grave

Ferguson 36.07474° -81.38151°

Hang your head, Tom Dula, they even got your name wrong. For the song anyway.

In July of 1866 a man named Tom Hall went to the house of James Grayson asking for work so he could earn enough money to buy some shoes. Little did Grayson know that Tom Hall was not the man's real name, and was instead Tom Dula, a man on the run. Little did Dula know that about a week later, Grayson would be the one to capture him.

Hours after Tom Dula left Grayson's farm, a group came to Grayson saying they were looking for a man named Tom Dula. Dula was wanted for the murder of Laura Foster, killed on June 18. The description they gave matched Tom Hall. Grayson joined the posse and went to get the local sheriff. The sheriff was not located so the group went looking on their own. After searching the area they found Dula soaking his feet in a stream. The new shoes he bought were not broken in and were giving him blisters.

Grayson arrested Dula without having to pull his pistol. At least not until having to discourage the rest of the posse from stringing Tom up then and there. Grayson then took Dula to Wilkes County to get a fair trial.

Tom was found guilty in 1868 and hanged in Statesville.

Moving ahead to 1929, James Grayson's nephew Gilliam Grayson and Henry Whittier went to Memphis to record *The Ballad of Tom Dooley*. Many versions of the song exist, but the Tom Dooley legend took hold in 1958 when a version of the song done by the Kingston Trio became a hit. That's the end of the story.

The beginning is something else entirely.

Tom Dula came back home from a Union prison camp after the Civil War to be with his sweetheart Anne Melton. It didn't seem to matter to him, or her, that she was already married to James Melton. Tom also slept with Anne's cousin Pauline Foster, who was being treated for syphilis, and then with Laura Foster, another cousin, who probably contracted the disease from Dula. Dula also gave the disease to Anne.

Laura then stole her father's horse and disappeared. She may have left to run away with Tom, or because of the shame and stigma of her disease. Her father was gravely concerned, for the horse. He didn't care if he ever saw his daughter again. And he wouldn't.

The horse came back, but no Laura.

Months later, Pauline accused Anne and Tom of killing Laura, leading people to the body, where she said Anne told her they buried the corpse. Laura had been stabbed once, through the heart.

After Dula's capture, the trial became a national news sensation, with The New York Times covering the case and former governor Zebulon Vance defending Dula. After two years of struggles in the court system, Tom was found guilty. Tom Dula wrote out a confession the day before his hanging, admitting he did it alone, with Anne having no hand in the crime. But on the wagon before he was hanged, his last words purportedly were, "I didn't harm a hair on the girl's head."

Many people think Anne killed Laura in a fit of jealousy because she was about to elope with Dula. Maybe Anne's husband James Melton framed Dula. Dula may actually have done it himself, angry at her for expecting him to run away or for telling of his romantic entanglements to Anne, or because he suspected Laura of giving him syphilis. Maybe it was someone else entirely. Who knows?

Hang your head, Tom Dula, hang your head.

Oddity ★★

Tom Dula's grave is chipped up so much from souvenir hunters that it looks like someone took a bite out of it.

Difficulty ★★

The grave is a ways up Tom Dula Road, and impossible to spot from the road due to high earthen banks along the side of the road. About 2/10ths of a mile from the grave is a path that leads to a gate in a fence. Walking up to the fence will lead to an overgrown path that goes to the gravesite. The path is very weedy, overgrown, muddy, and you don't know what, or who, you may run into. Long pants and hiking boots, something you don't mind getting dirty, are recommended. There are lots of No Trespassing signs up, but technically, they are posted for the other side of the fence. Dula's grave is often said to be on private property, but there really don't seem to be any signs there. That doesn't mean you won't be prosecuted, though. Go at your own risk, and definitely don't take souvenirs!

Anne Melton died two years after Tom Dula's trial, having gone insane, most likely from the syphilis. Near Dula's grave is a chicken farm with the words on the side, "Disease is a Killer!"

It is often noted that Tom Dula has a different name than Tom Dooley. That is because it is part of Appalachian speech to pronounce the "a" as a "y". This is obvious in the change of the word "opera" in "The Grand Ole Opry."

Laura Foster's grave is up the road on 268, buried into the hill on the edge of a property line in a cow pasture. The grave is shored up by rail ties and surrounded by a small white fence.
See it at 36.04978° -81.44605°.

Mystery Hill

Blowing Rock 36.16345° -81.64420°

There is very little that can said about Mystery Hill that isn't already hyped, er, said, by Mystery Hill itself. Mystery Hill, you see, is part of a vortex, a whirlpool of energy that changes gravity, turns things sideways, and makes people grow right in front of your eyes!

Mystery Hill has several attractions on its site. The tour begins with the history of Mystery Hill, which originally was an apple orchard. Workers noticed that one of the twin brothers that worked lifting bushels of apples would appear taller than the other, even though they were standing on level ground. It didn't matter which one it was, the one closer to the hill always seemed taller. They also discovered a vortex along the hill during apple harvest time. Instead of collecting the apples under the trees, the workers tried to roll them downhill, but the apples would always roll toward one side of the hill, not straight down.

So now, visitors can experience these same strange forces that the apple orchard's workers discovered. Outside is the Mystery Platform, a level slab of concrete built into the hillside where the person on the north side of the platform appears taller than the person on the south side. Shorter people can actually look taller than people who normally have a few inches on them anywhere else. Visitors can even watch a person grow as they walk across the flat concrete.

While the Mystery Platform has a certain appeal, the Mystery House is the main attraction here. Built upon the location of the mysterious vortex, visitors find it impossible to stand upright in the Mystery House. Guests to the house begin leaning at a 45° angle, due to the "stronger than average pull to the north," as Mystery Hill claims. Inside, there are many ways to experience the strange vortex that is Mystery Hill. Guests can sit in a swing that flies up to the ceiling on the backswing, and then stops halfway through its motion, never going up through the rest of the swing. A ball will roll uphill inside the house, a truly odd sight, and guests can even see water run uphill instead of down.

The Mystery House does have an obvious slant downward to it, which can explain why people lean forward in an almost precarious way, but when you visit, there really is an odd, uncomfortable sensation that you get just standing in the room.

In addition to the Mystery House, there is the Hall of Mystery, which includes puzzles and experiments for kids, and fun-loving adults, to try. There are several soap bubble experiments to play with, including one bubble big enough to stand inside.

Mystery Hill has grown over time from just a freaky vortex site that gets visitors to stop for a few minutes to let the kids run around into a pretty interesting place to visit. In 1989 the Appalachian Heritage Museum was added to the site. Originally it was located on the campus of Appalachian State University and known as the Dougherty House, it was moved to Mystery Hill to display Appalachian antiques from the 19th century. The building itself is rather important in that it was not only one of the first buildings built on the ASU campus, it was also the first building in the county to have water and electricity.

Most likely, the kids are going to want to spend all their time in the Mystery House, trying out the strange vortex gravity field inside the house. And who could blame them? To put it simply, this place is freaky. You have to experience this.

Oddity ★★★★

Hold on to something so you don't float away.

Difficulty ★

You can't miss the signs for Mystery Hill as you drive toward the mountains. It's right on Highway 321. If you need an excuse while you're in Blowing Rock or Boone, just say the gravity pulled you there.

Land of Oz

Beech Mountain   36.18456° -81.88184°

The dream of Tweetsie Railroad owner Grover Robbins and Charlotte designer Jack Pentes was to finally create what fans of the Oz books had wanted for decades. Ever since the books first became popular, readers of L. Frank Baum's series have wanted to be able to walk into the real Land of Oz. In 1970, that's what Robbins did.

With the design help of Pentes, Robbins created a faithful and fanciful version of the Land of Oz from the books Robbins even encouraged his employees not to see the movie, but read the books instead. The Land of Oz was meant to employ workers from the Beech Mountain ski slopes during the warmer seasons. It was designed to be different than a regular amusement park, with more of an experience or tour rather than waiting in lines for the Oz Scrambler ride.

Visitors would start at Dorothy's house where they got to experience being caught in a twister, with Auntie Em encouraging them to get down to the cellar. While inside they saw the tornado emerge, from a discretely placed projector, while witches appeared on the walls. After the storm was over, everyone went safely up a secret door that Dorothy must have known of, only to find that the house is all disheveled from being spun around in the tornado. When the guests left the house by the back door they discovered that the whole house has landed them on a path taking them to the outskirts of Oz. They, like Dorothy, would meet the Scarecrow, the Tin Woodsman, and the Cowardly Lion. The Wicked Witch of the West was there as well, and the yellow brick road led to the Emerald City. The Land of Oz had original musical numbers that the visitors got to hear, along with the classic "Over The Rainbow." Guests finished their tour with a gondola balloon ride over the park, leaving Oz like the wizard before them.

The Land of Oz operated from 1970 to 1980. When it first opened, Oz was very successful, but after a few years, the park lost its popularity with increased travel costs and a downturn in the economy that kept people away. In 1976, the Emerald City caught fire, burning several of the costumes, including an original dress worn by Dorothy in the movie. By 1980, the park was closed and fell into disrepair, with vandals and the elements taking their toll.

Not until ten years later did some of the former cast begin to take an interest in the property. They began Autumn at Oz first as a reunion, which later became an annual event for fans of Oz and the park. Now, the first weekend of October opens the gate to Oz for a glimpse into the past, and a little bit into the future. The park is finally getting restored little by little. Guests can rent Dorothy's house, complete with wicked witch feet underneath and the feeling of a cyclone in the basement. Some of the original munchkin homes have been preserved, and a few of the talking trees are still visible. The property developer has restored one balloon gondola, probably the only one still in existence. The Emerald City may be gone, but the yellow brick road still is there. So now, once a year, fans can still be off to see the wizard.

Oddity ★★★★

So Oz was in North Carolina? In the mountains?

Difficulty ★★★

It takes a twisty drive up to Beech Mountain at only one time a year to see the Land of Oz. You need to plan in advance and get tickets for the tour. This is a very popular event, and lines are usually very long to get in.

You can rent out Dorothy's house or take a private tour of Oz now, through Emerald Mountain Realty and Rentals.

Jack Pentes designed the Land of Oz from a child's point of view. He got down on his knees to visualize what it would look like from a kid's eyes. In order to preserve the natural beauty, Pentes did not spoil the landscape. He cut down only one tree in the whole park.

Jack Pentes was an artist and designer in Charlotte. He also was Bobo the clown on Big Bill's Club House on WBTV back in 1957.

Brown Mountain Lights

Highway 181 overlook near Morganton 35.94250° -81.84205°

Wiseman's View Linville Falls 35.90324° -81.90749°

Lost Cove Cliffs Pineola 36.02902° -81.87175°

The oldest, most well known and most mysterious lights of North Carolina are the Brown Mountain Lights. These mysterious lights have been seen since the 1200s. The first explorer to the region, Gerard de Brahm, saw them all the way back in 1771. The lights have been seen before the Civil War, before electric lights, before automobiles or flashlights. They have essentially been seen since way before the advent of any useful bright portable light system that could be used to create these lights. And they are still seen to this day.

The lights are not common, and can appear in different ways. The lights sometimes appear twice as big as stars in the sky, and are mainly red or white in color, but other colors appear as well. The balls of light form in the trees on the mountainside, and will rise up over the mountain. The lights usually appear for about 10 seconds or less, but some may last longer, up to a minute or more. They have even been seen splitting apart or joining together in the sky over Brown Mountain.

The theories for the cause of the Brown Mountain Lights are many, but none really fit with the reality of their existence. Numerous ghost stories are attached to the lights, including an old tale that recounts a battle between the Cherokee and Catawba tribes, where a large number of braves on both sides were killed in the fight. After the battle, women from both tribes searched the mountainside with torches in order to recover the missing bodies of their men. The legend is that the lights are the tragic battle's aftermath being reenacted by the spirits of maidens still searching for their lost warriors.

Other legends include the ghost of a devoted slave searching for his master, lost while hunting on the mountain. Then there is the story of a woman murdered by her husband in around 1850. The lights are the spirit of the woman, telling people to stop searching for her. These two legends, even taking into account the supernatural aspect of the tales, do not consider that the lights had been seen before the events of these legends actually happened.

Many theories insist that the lights are some sort of gas flare up, like foxfire or will-o-the-wisp. The lights, however, do not appear as gas fires, like a flame, but more as glowing orbs. They also move and are not stationary to some sort of exhaust. Other ideas include uranium deposits, or pitchblende, glowing off in the dark. Also suggested were the reflections of lights from nearby Lenoir and Hickory, or from railroad locomotive lights, despite the fact that people were seeing the lights before electric lights were in Hickory or Lenoir, or that the lights have been seen when the railroad had been washed out for weeks. There may also be some tie in to magnetic shifts in the earth's crust, or a proximity to fault lines.

Seeing the lights is not always easy. They do not appear every night. In fact, they seem finicky about when they want to appear. The lights appear more often in the early fall, from September through October. They have been seen from sunset to sunrise, but are more prominent from 10 pm to 2 am. Moonless nights with clear skies obviously are better for spotting the lights. But some watchers say to look either during a light rain or soon after a rain. (Please note that the photo is an artist's interpretation of what the lights might look like.)

But why worry about specific times of the year and spoil a good night out? Take a thermos and some snacks, enjoy the lights.

Oddity

If you see them, they are one of the strangest things to spot in the whole state. You get to see something no one has explained.

Difficulty ★★★

Getting to one of the overlooks to see the lights is fairly easy, but the road will be a little twisty in the mountains. Be aware that you will have to stay up late, on a dark mountain with no services. And there's no guarantee that the lights will appear.

The Brown Mountain overlook is on Highway 181, about 20.5 miles north of Morganton which starts as North Green Street in the town. The overlook is marked as an area to see Brown Mountain, and includes a tablet that describes the Brown Mountain Lights. The overlook also seems to include about every single flying bug in the state.

Wiseman's View is off of Old NC 105, near Linville. There is a viewing ledge for the gorge. This is much farther away. Look to the east into the gorge and along the ridge toward Brown Mountain.

The Lost Cove Cliffs overlook on the Blue Ridge Parkway has a direct view of Brown Mountain, but it often gets overgrown, and the view may be obscured by plant life.

Quilt Block Vertical Sundial

Burnsville 35.91829°   -82.29947°

Throughout Mitchell and Yancey counties in the western part of North Carolina there are a number of quilt trails where painted blocks with quilt designs hang on barns, houses, and businesses throughout the region. There are currently over 200 quilt designs and the number is still growing. Each design is unique, usually to its owner, and is never duplicated. Many of the patterns are in classic quilt patterns, but some are quite distinctive. For example, the local Chevrolet dealership in Burnsville has a '65 Corvette pattern. Among the different patterns are coffee pots, baseball fields, a circular saw for a lumber company, a coat hanger star for a dry cleaner, bulldozers, and a boat and paddle at a rafting business.

The most unique of them all hangs in Burnsville at the office of the Yancey Commons Times Journal. The quilt block is unusual in that it is also a sundial, and a vertical sundial at that. It hangs on the side of their building, unlike most sundials that sit flat on the ground. If that wasn't enough, the designers made sure that an object that told time was installed with perfect timing. The quilt block sundial was installed on May 19, 2010, which was the 100 year anniversary of the use of time zones. May 20, the day it was dedicated, was the first day of Spring and National Quilting Day.

The sundial has several very interesting features. The stars at the top show their position in the sky on the night of December 29, 1833, the day when Yancey County was founded. The three rows of numbers show the old local time before the advent of time zones, Eastern Standard Time, and Eastern Daylight Time.

Of course, the best feature is the beauty and peculiarity of a giant vertical sundial hanging on the side of a building. Stand back, check the time, enjoy the view.

Oddity ★★★

The sundial was conceived and designed by Bob Hampton, a Yancy County resident, as well as sundial maker and astronomer. Quilt Trails says this is the only quilt block sundial in existence. Also, it is the largest vertical sundial in North Carolina. So, just where are the others?

Difficulty ★

The sundial hangs near the middle of Burnsville, right off of the town square, on the side of the Yancy Common Times Journal building.

At the bottom of the sundial is the equation of time. It shows how much time to add or subtract to change sun time to clock time. During the year the sun time fluctuates as much as 14 to 16 minutes off of clock time, so you add or subtract... Oh, just say it's lunch time and go get a sandwich.

Andrews Geyser

Old Fort 35.65109° -82.24168°

Andrews Geyser sits on Mill Creek Road off of US 70 to the west of Old Fort. The fountain was built in 1885 after a rather amazing feat of railroad engineering. Originally, the Western North Carolina rail line stopped at Old Fort because no one could quite figure how to run the tracks through the mountains to Asheville. Colonel Alexander Boyd Andrews lead the push to run the train into the mountains, and the fountain is named after him.

After finishing the line, the fountain was built in front of the Round Knob Hotel, partly as a tribute to the approximately 120 people who died building the railroad, and partly as a landmark that would entice people to get off the train at the hotel. The fountain was situated so that its towering spray can be seen several times along the railway line.

The Andrews Geyser is not a natural geyser; rather, it is gravity fed from a dam higher up on the mountain at the Inn on Mill Creek. Yes, the geyser can be turned on and off! It starts as a 6 inch pipe that narrows down to ½ inch at the geyser. During the winter, the water freezes at the base, making an ice hill of up to 50 feet, and in the summer the spray makes a continual rainbow.

Andrews Geyser sits in the middle of a park with several picnic tables and some shady areas nearby. Shady, as in tree lined and cool, that is. This is well worth the drive for a nice outdoor lunch stop.

Oddity ★★

In man's conquest over nature to build a railroad track through the mountains, a tribute was made with a man-made geyser.

Difficulty ★

This is only a few miles off of I-40, but it is up a mountain road. In front of the geyser is a gravel parking area, but the road drops off a little bit onto the gravel. Some spots are not great for parking if you have a low sports car.

The Round Knob Hotel burned down in 1903, and the geyser fell into disrepair over time. The geyser was restored by George Fisher Baker, who was a friend of Andrews, in 1911. But due to its location near the rail line, the railroad company would not grant an easement for the fountain, so the geyser, piping, and nozzle were moved across the creek where the new (current) basin was constructed.

If you want to see why building a railroad into the mountains was such a big deal, look at Andrews Geyser from an overhead view, like an aerial photo. The railroad does an amazing 10 plus curves (depending on how you count them) in the area around the geyser.

The Urban Trail

Asheville 35.59500° -82.55161°

There are plenty of hiking trails throughout the mountains of Buncombe County. If you need a workout, or just a chance to get back to nature, you will have no problem finding a place to trek. But what if you are a hip urbanite You want a hot latté with your walk? Or maybe you are just less inclined to get out into the wild?

You take the Urban Trail.

The Urban Trail began in 1991 as a way to showcase Asheville's history and its present beauty. The trail is only 1.7 miles long, and can be shortened into sections. The walk is divided into historical parts for different areas of the city, with some famous landmarks as stops along the way. Five different time periods are marked by icons in pink granite embedded into the sidewalks. There is a horseshoe representing the Frontier period, a feather for the Guilded Age, an angel, appropriately, for the Times of Thomas Wolfe, a courthouse for the Era of Civic Pride, and the Age of Diversity is represented by an eagle. Thirty sculptures mark the historic spots of the trail. Some stick out and are easily noticeable, such as the wild turkeys at Pack Place, or the giant iron representing the Flat Iron Building. There are others that are more subtle, like the top hat and cane on the bench where the Grand Opera House once stood, or a replica of Thomas Wolfe's shoes in front of his mother's boarding house. One of the most unique pieces is called On The Move, a sculpture with a wheel that turns to activates a sound system to play 11 different sounds related to transportation and how moving around the city changed over the years.

The Urban Trail is a self guided walking trail, owned by the city and managed by the Asheville Arts Council. Stop by the Asheville Art Museum, next to Pack Plaza, for a guide map. Then get walking.

Oddity ★★

Some of the landmarks are very creative and different. You will want to keep moving to the next one.

Difficulty ★★★

Hiking in the city isn't too hard, with only a little elevation change and plenty of places to stop and rest. Be aware that the trail is 1.7 miles and dress for the weather.

Lake Lure Church Bell

Lake Lure 35.43311° -82.19573°

Lake Lure is definitely one of the most beautiful places you'll ever see in North Carolina. National Geographic named it one of the top ten man-made lakes in the world. When you visit, you have to wonder, "Why not number one?"

Lucius Morse and his family bought what is now Lake Lure, as well as nearby Chimney Rock in 1902. The lake was created in 1927 by building a dam that made electric power for the Morse family to sell to the Blue Ridge Power company. When the lake was impounded, Elizabeth Morse, Lucius' wife, gave it the name Lake Lure, because the lake was so alluring.

But before the lake was formed, there was a town of a few homes and a church in the valley. The town of Buffalo was purchased, lock, stock and barrel, and the former owners were moved out, quite possibly with only what they could carry. While some of the buildings were removed or destroyed, parts of the town sit preserved at the bottom of Lake Lure, the cold, still, clean waters protecting the town from decay. There was even a farm truck, an REO Speedwagon, pulled from the lake after a resident of the original town told where he had left it when the lake was formed. The magneto still worked, so it was cleaned up, and fired up, and painted red. It is used now as the Buffalo Fire Dept. truck in local parades.

But the spooky thing really is the old town. It sits preserved in the cold waters, glass still in the windows, colored glaze still on the church's windowpanes. And a bell still in the church steeple. It is said that if one takes a boat out to the middle of the lake at midnight, the church bell can be heard tolling from under the water, with ghosts ringing the bell to call back the residents of Buffalo.

Is it ghosts ringing the bell? Spirits of the displaced wanting to come back for one more Sunday? Spectral relatives visiting the church's graveyard? Or is it just an underwater current stirring the bell? Go out at night on the still waters of Lake Lure and see for yourself.

Oddity ★★★★

Underneath the still beauty of Lake Lure hides a great story, and a great legend.

Difficulty ★★★★★

You will at the very least need a boat to get out to the lake at midnight. Underwater microphones optional. You want to actually see it? That water gets cold when it gets deep, so scuba diving is probably a bad idea. At 35.43492° -82.23148° is the local visitor's center, as well as the boat rental and ramp. Lake Lure Tours rents boats for daily use, if you want to go out at midnight to listen for the bell. Just be aware that cruising on the lake at night can be unsafe.

In addition to the church bell, there are legends of "little people" who used to live in the valley, a rumbling mountain, and battles of giant horsemen in the clouds.

Lake Lure celebrates its movie heritage with a Dirty Dancing Weekend at the end of Summer with movie showings, dance competitions, and craft vendors. The original dance floor from the movie was saved and moved into the lobby of the nearby Esmeralda Inn located in Chimney Rock..

Morris the Tryon Horse

Tryon 35.20848° -82.23817°

Tryon had brushes with greatness from a lot of people, including a governor, a singer, and a consulting detective. But a horse may be the most important to the residents.

Morris the horse is a long time landmark for the little mountain town, nestled between the Smokies and the Blue Ridge. Morris is a large version of a toy rocking horse originally made by the Tryon Toy-Makers and Wood Carvers. The Toy-Makers and Wood Carvers group was started by two ladies, Eleanor Vance and Charlotte Yale, when they moved from Asheville to Tryon. They had been teaching wood carving to young boys near Biltmore, supported at the time by Edith Vanderbilt.  They continued their work when they moved to Tryon by starting the Toy-Makers and Wood Carvers craft organization in Tryon in 1915. One of their most popular toys was a wooden rocking horse. Vance designed a large version in 1928, and Meredith Lankford and Odell Peeler from the craft organization built the original giant horse for the Tryon Riding and Hunt Club.

There have been four (or five, depending how you count them) different versions of Morris. The first, created by the Toy- Makers and Wood Carvers, was a much larger version than the current horse. That horse was lost in a fire when the building in which it was stored burned down. The second horse was essentially destroyed when it was stolen by drunken revelers. A third horse replaced the destroyed one and it lived a long wooden life before being worn down by the weather in the 1960s. A fourth horse was built to replace the third one. When it was worn out, the horse was refurbished with a fiberglass body, and now sits in the center of town.

The current Morris the horse is used as a town billboard, announcing events and happenings around Tryon, including events at the Tryon Riding and Hunt Club. He is often dressed up for the season or special events. Morris gets his name from an article run occasionally by the Tryon Daily Bulletin, where Morris has a conversation with one of the readers. He was referred to as Morris by the Wilderness Road Gang, a group of locals who dress the horse every year in garlands and a top hat for Christmas.

Oddity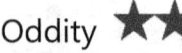

Residents use the horse as a landmark. "Go past the horse, turn left."

Difficulty ★

The original surveyors of Tryon placed a compass on the map and drew a circle to represent the boundary of Tryon. Morris the horse sits at the middle of the circle, so he is literally in the center of the town.

William Gillette, the first person to portray Sherlock Holmes on stage, lived in Tryon. As did singer Nina Simone.

Harry's Grille and Piggy's Ice

Hendersonville 35.33120° -82.44956°

Piggy's Ice was opened in 1980 by Harry Thompson. His wife, "Piggy," made it very clear that she was not going to be scooping ice cream there. But when the stand was ready to open, Harry was still working his other job, so Piggy went to work. Since business was doing so well, Harry decided to build a restaurant next door. Sadly, Harry passed away while the building was being built, but it opened in 1993, and was named in honor of him.

Many people go to Harry's Grille for the barbecue sandwiches or to Piggy's for the 20 flavors of ice cream, but what makes this place novel is the plethora of strange statues and advertising figures on the roof and inside the buildings.

On the roof of the two buildings sit pink elephants, a Big Boy holding an apple, a cow, a giant ice cream cone, Yogi and Boo Boo, an Esso or Exxon Tiger, a Burger Chef statue, an Officer Big Mac head, and a giant bull head, among other things.

Inside it gets better. There's a Hooterville jail, and statues of Colonel Sanders and Ronald McDonald. And the most important part. Some of the tastiest burgers and shakes in North Carolina.

Oddity ★★★

It's nice when someone preserves classic Americana. It's scary when they start to have an army.

Difficulty ★

If you can't find the giant Yogi Bear on the corner in Hendersonville, you deserve to go hungry! It's right on 7th Avenue east, near Highway 64.

Look Homeward Angel Statue

Hendersonville 35.31963° -82.47482°

In 1929, Thomas Wolfe wrote *Look Homeward Angel*, a fictionalized autobiography of his life growing up in Asheville. The novel tells the story of Eugene Gant and how he grew up in the fictional town of Altamont. The statue of the story sat on the porch of Gant's home as he grew up. Wolfe would have seen the real statue at his father's workplace.

Thomas Wolfe's father, W.O. Wolfe, was a gravestone salesman in Asheville. He sold the statue to the Johnson family as a marker for their family's gravesite in Oakdale Cemetery in Hendersonville. The statue greatly resembles the description that Wolfe wrote in his first, autobiographical, novel, *Look Homeward Angel*, where Wolfe refers to the angel as holding a stone lily in her hand, and standing on the ball of her foot.

The statue sits in Oakdale Cemetery near downtown Hendersonville. The angel can be viewed easily, and is surrounded by a wrought iron fence marking the Johnson family plot.

Oddity ★

The statue is both beautiful and sad. Viewing it will give the visitor a similar feeling that Eugene Gant had in the book.

Difficulty ★

Read the book *Look Homeward, Angel* before going out to find this. The cemetery is off Highway 64/6th Avenue West in Hendersonville. There are several turnoffs into the cemetery.

The inscription on the statue reads...
Margaret E. Wife of H. F. Johnson Born May 13, 1882
Died at Brookhaven, Miss.
May 26, 1905,
"Her Children Arise Up and Call Her Blessed" Our Mother

Ten miles down the road is another grave marker of note. The world's largest twins are buried in a nearby graveyard at Crab Creek Baptist Church.

PARI Radio Telescopes

Rosman 35.19996° -82.87236°

"We need a place to promote science." – Don Cline.

Don Cline founded the Pisgah Astronomical Research Institute (PARI) in 1998, preserving a piece of scientific history and creating a campus for the study of astronomy. Today, PARI offers scientific study to students of all ages, from elementary through college.

PARI was originally built by NASA in 1962 and named the Rosman Research Station. It was used as the primary satellite tracking facility of the east coast throughout NASA's heyday of the '60s and through the Apollo and Skylab years. The location 30 miles out of Asheville in the Pisgah National Forest was chosen for its remoteness. The national forest preserved the area around Rosman as a place never to be tainted with all the things that limit astronomy. Being built in the middle of nowhere meant no light pollution and no radio signal interference. No businesses, no radio signals, no streetlights, no orange glow in the night sky would ever spoil the perfect sky above Rosman.

NASA built several instruments at Rosman, including the two huge 26 meter radio telescopes that are easily noticeable when visiting. There are several other radio telescopes, as well as optical telescopes along the Optical Ridge.

NASA operated the site until 1981, when the increased money placed in the space shuttle program and newer satellites meant that Rosman was no longer needed by NASA. In 1981 it was turned over to the Department of Defense and the National Security Agency ran the site for 14 years. In that time, the NSA did some serious improvements to the site. They built several new buildings and updated many of the facilities. They also added fences and guards. NSA wanted the area to be self sufficient so they created two of everything on the site, so that there was a backup to every part of Rosman, including two wells for water and two generators. The NSA's additions meant that Rosman had power enough for a small city. The security was so tight that a fisherman who once wandered onto the woods near the property was promptly caught and questioned for an hour.

By 1995, the facility was closed down and left to the Forest Service. Most of the antennas and secret electronics from the NSA days were moved to other areas, but the buildings, fiber optic cables, and other upgrades remained at the site. The Forest Service continued to maintain the facility for a while, but decided to raze the structures and let the area return to forest, as it was costing too much money for the upkeep.

In 1998, after seeing the value in the equipment and the location, Don Cline created a non-profit group that bought the facilities and founded the Pisgah Astronomical Research Institute. The group began the restoration of the equipment to turn the place into an educational campus for primary through college students and schools. Today the campus contains several radio telescopes, along with optical telescopes, a solar antenna, and several weather and environmental monitoring devices. They offer services to schools and universities, including remote access via the internet to their 4.6 meter radio telescope, named Smiley due to the big smiling face painted on the dish. Students will also attend weeklong classes at PARI building telescopes and doing NASA research projects. They offer classes for homeschooled students and programs on robotics as well as astronomy.

PARI does pure research as well as student based classes at its site. One of the programs done at PARI is a research project run by Dan Reichart from Morehead Planetarium at UNC-Chapel Hill. The program, called SKYNET, links telescopes around the world with a satellite that is searching for gamma ray bursts, so that when the satellite detects a burst, the telescopes immediately turn toward the area where the gamma rays were detected. Telescopes begin immediately taking pictures of the area in order to document not only the gamma ray bursts, but also the first visible signs, the first optical moments or afterglow of ultraviolet, x-ray, or radio bursts that occur during these brief bursts.

The PARI campus offers planetarium shows, tours, and star parties to people visiting the institute. Visitors are welcome Monday through Friday from 9 am to 4 pm, with guided tours most Wednesdays at 2 pm. Among the things to see include the Galaxy Walk, a representation of our solar system in scale, the PARI Museum and the gift shop. PARI has an evening tour on the second Friday of every month, where visitors can look though telescopes to view the heavens on clear nights.

PARI has also become important as a historical site. Their Astronomical Photographic Data Archive contains a large number of significant photos and documents from the history of the U.S. space program. The collection has about 100,000 images on glass, negatives, and prints. Some of the images are over 100 years old. The collection also houses about 56,000 images of meteors that had been collected from the 1930s to the 1970s by Harvard and the Smithsonian.

The collection of photos holds an important historical aspect, but the most visible part of PARI is a rare and important artifact as well. The massive 26 meter east radio telescope was the first of its kind ever constructed.

Oddity ★★

PARI is a rare and historical part of North Carolina. Maybe that's why they don't let anyone skateboard in the big dishes.

Difficulty ★★

PARI is located north of Rosman between the town and Balsam Grove on Highway 215. It is far up in the mountains, and they do charge for organized tours. But it's for a good cause. It might be easier to get there in a flying saucer, but most people don't have one in their garage, so driving would be the safe bet.

NSA was so secretive that it was said the initials stood for "No Such Agency".

The Smiley dish was painted with its distinctive face during PARI's NSA days, when the Soviets would use satellites to spy on the NSA's listening post. That way, the Russians had something looking back up at them.

Bear Shadow

Cashiers 35.09842° -83.15056°

There is a well known tale that is told around the areas of Cashiers and Highlands about a bear that comes out of hibernation every autumn. When the sun sets behind Whiteside Mountain, it casts a bear-like shadow onto the fall colored valley below. The bear shadow slowly stretches out into the wooded land over a half an hour or more until the sun finally sets in the west. The shadow is visible in the fall from mid-October to early November. The most popular area to view the shadow is on Rhodes Big View Overlook on Highway 64. The overlook is about 4.3 miles west of the stoplight in Cashiers. The shadow of the bear starts to form around 5:30 pm and lasts for about half an hour.

There's more to do in Jackson County than just seeing the bear. This is a great place to see the fall foliage, as well as go fishing or hiking. Whiteside Mountain, which forms the shadow, has beautiful sheer cliffs that give the mountain its name. Visitors can stay in a rustic cabin or at a resort, and use either as a base to check out the numerous waterfalls in the area. And as the day grows long, the downtown area of Highlands offers shopping and restaurants.

Oddity ★★★★

There's no need for any honey or a picnic basket to coax this bear out.

Difficulty ★★★

Several things make this difficult to view. The bear only appears on clear days. It only happens at two times during the year. And, due to the popularity of the view, Rhodes Big View overlook on Highway 64 gets crowded with photographers and other viewers. Get there a little early.

The bear shadow can also be seen in late winter from mid February to early March.

Judaculla Rock

Cullowhee 35.30085° -83.10982°

In ancient times, a Cherokee legend tells that Tsul'kalu', the slant eyed giant, while stepping down from a mountaintop to a creek, reached out with his seven fingered hand to steady himself and scratched several strange images into the soapstone rock now known as Judaculla (being an evolution from the name Tsul'kalu').

It probably is as good a story as anything else for this strange rock. Even the Cherokee consider it ancient before their time. The best date put to the Judaculla rock carvings is somewhere from 3000 to 1000 BC, based on soapstone bowls being made at about the same time.

The strangeness of the rock created more modern legends, including the use of the area for rituals among students at Western Carolina University for initiations into student groups or orders at the school. Others report ghostly noises at night or visits from UFOs. These tales just makes the place all the more odd.

The petroglyphs themselves are unique in that the shapes do not seem to have any truly recognizable pattern or meaning. To this day, no one has determined what they mean, or the reason for putting the markings on the rock in the first place. In the 1930s, a famous photograph of Judaculla Rock was taken, showing all the petroglyphs filled in with chalk in order to highlight the carvings. It has later been discovered that using chalk to illuminate the petroglyphs actually increases the wear on them, making them disappear faster. However, since the rock is exposed, the glyphs have been eroding steadily, and the only evidence we may have of the carvings on Judaculla Rock in the future will be that photo. Even high contrast photos today, such as the one shown here, only bring out the basic holes and lines of the rock.

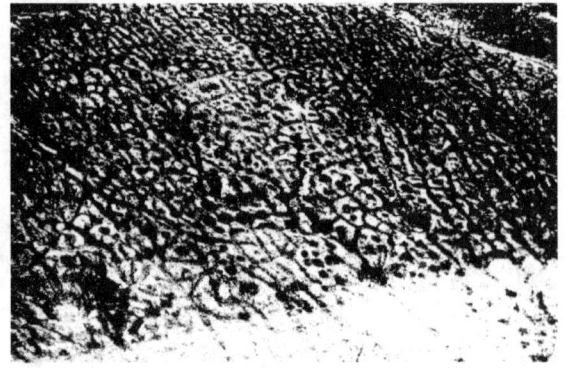

Judaculla Rock is owned by Jackson County. There currently is a stand around the rock for people to walk on, but no cover over it to protect the rock from the elements. As such, the petroglyphs in the soft soapstone are slowly wearing away. Sooner or later, the visible rock will be worn smooth by rain and snow, so see it now.

Oddity ★★★★

See if you can read it. Maybe there's a comics section.

Difficulty ★★

The rock is on a dirt road in the middle of nearly nowhere. It's off of Judaculla Road, a branch off of Caney Fork Road near Cullowhee. There is no dedicated parking, but there is an area where a few cars can pull off the road near a walkway that takes visitors down to the rock. It would be better to park as far away as possible and walk to the rock, as car exhaust increases the erosion of the petroglyphs.

The Fugitive Train Wreckage

Dillsboro 35.37006° -83.26318°

In *The Fugitive*, a 1993 movie starring Harrison Ford, Richard Kimble, a Chicago surgeon, is falsely accused of murdering his wife. During a bus transport to his death row prison cell, the other prisoners attempt to escape, killing the bus driver. A guard, while trying to stop the prisoners, fires his shotgun into the swaying bus floor, shooting through the floorboard, and blowing out the tire. The bus hits a guardrail, tumbles over the edge and rolls to a stop on the train tracks below. As if that wasn't bad enough, while Kimble is trying to help an injured guard, a train comes down the tracks, barreling toward the bus and the helpless occupants inside.

A guard and prisoner abandon Kimble, so on his own, he lifts the wounded man and throws him out the window, saving the guard's life. Kimble jumps at the last second, while the train plows into the bus carcass, then derails and chases him down until he jumps out of the way at the last moment.

A lot of the action is just special effects, but the train wreck was real.

The remnants of the wreck sit by the tracks outside of Dillsboro. The rail line is used by the Great Smoky Mountains Railroad for scenic and holiday train tours. Their train runs right by the wreckage, which either might need some explaining, or might be the highlight of the ride.

Next to the line sits both the train engines as well as the bus that got slammed in the movie. The film was supposed to be taking place in Illinois, as Kimble was from Chicago, so the train was painted up in Illinois Southern red, gray, and yellow. While the trains are a little rusty now, they still have a bit of their color left.

The wreckage is visible from the road only during the winter, when there are no leaves on the trees. However, there is no pull off area above the wreck, so stopping on the road is unsafe. The best view is from a ride on the tracks on the Great Smoky Mountains Railroad. If you don't want to do that, most of the wreck is visible from across the river. Taking the bridge over the river to Macktown Road will lead to Tunnel Mountain Road. This dirt road runs right next to the river, up to a small group of trailers on, believe it or not, Fugitive Run. There is no parking available there, but the wreckage is more visible.

Oddity ★★★

It's kind of weird to leave a train wreck right there where people riding by on trains can see it.

Difficulty ★★

The wreck is off the road and the best way to see the wreckage is to take the GSMR on one of their rides. The area is also accessible by kayak from the Tukaseegee River. There is no access from the road directly, as there is a fence along the road. Stay off the rails and watch for passing trains. Dr. Kimble won't be there to save you.

Movie scenes at the hospital were filmed in Sylva at the Harris Regional Hospital. Kimble jumped from Cheoah Dam near Tapoco. And, if you look close, you'll see a road sign for Murphy in the film.

Santa's Land Theme Park

Cherokee   35.46753° -83.26472°

Santa's Land is a family theme park based on, well, Santa's Land. Welcome to the North Pole, Cherokee style. Yes, it has rides, but no rollercoaster. It has a Rudicoaster. As in Rudolph, the Red Nosed Reindeer. Ride a rollercoaster with a giant reindeer head, complete with antlers and red nose on the front car. Santa's Land has plenty of other rides, too, all geared toward Santa's little fans. Rides include a miniature train, kiddie cars, and paddle boats. There's also a Ferris Wheel and carousel that all can ride.

If that's not enough, Santa's Land has a petting zoo. You would expect to be able to feed the deer. More surprising would be to feed the lemurs. Take a boat out on Whitebeard's Lake, being sure you have a little monkey chow first, to feed the lemurs and the monkeys. If that's not enough, see them feed the baby bears three times a day. Add on llamas, kangaroos, peacocks, and a myriad other bunch of animals to create a real mountain menagerie.

If you get hungry, pick up a Rudi burger at Santa's Snack Bar. Don't worry, it's just a fun name, and not actually made from reindeer.

Is Santa at Santa's Land? Yes, every day. Well, every day May through October. He does have to get ready for the busy Christmas season at some time. No wonder they close by November. Kids can even fill out an envelope so that Santa will send them a letter before Christmas.

In the big world of giant megaparks, Santa's land is a quant throwback to a simple fun time for our children to come visit Old Saint Nick. Santa's Land is a wonderful place for little kids, and parents like it, too.

Oddity ★

Santa's Land has a classic look, with pretty unique attractions for the kids.

Difficulty ★

It is much easier to get to this North Pole than the other one. Admission fees are high, but guests get to spend a long time in Santa's Land, and food is relatively cheap and good.

The Chiefs of Cherokee

Cherokee 35.48477° -83.31601° (Museum of the Cherokee)

Cherokee is a dream come true for passersby of oddity, strangeness, and unique culture. There probably is no other place where one can see a casino resort, giant teepees, a huge arrowhead sign, get your picture with a chief, enjoy a stroll on a picturesque river, learn some incredible history, and see an outdoor play.

The mountains of western North Carolina have been the home of the Cherokee for as long as 11,000 years. There are even legends of Cherokee hunting mastodon before the enormous beasts went extinct. It took until 1838 for the Cherokee to be separated from their land. Even though for thousands of years the land offered abundant animals for hunting, plenty of crops, wood, shelter, plenty of fish, pottery and basketmaking, it took the federal government with its desire for the land for plantations and gold to push the Cherokee into Oklahoma.  Over 16,000 Cherokee would be sent west, with about 4000 dying along the way.

But some were able to stay. Some Cherokee were able to live off the land and avoid the roundup by the federal government, while about 400 Cherokee, the Oconaluftee, lived in the Great Smoky Mountains on a white man's land, and because they were on private land were able to stay. These and some others later became the Eastern Band of the Cherokee Nation.

In the 1930s, with the formation of the Great Smoky Mountains National Park, the boundary to the park became a popular tourist stop, with visitors looking for Cherokee souvenirs. Tourism grew in the 1950s and Cherokee grew with it. *Unto These Hills*, an outdoor historical drama about the history of the Cherokee up until their forced removal by the Trail of Tears, opened in 1950 to 100,000 visitors. With the uptick in tourism, many motels and gas stations opened in Cherokee.

In 1951, fortunate happenstance created one of the most enduring and popular icons of Cherokee. When Henry Lambert was 16, he was asked by a gift shop owner to fill in for his "chief," who stood for photos with tourists outside the shop. Lambert discovered that he made more money posing for pictures that week than he did working his usual construction job. For the next five decades, Chief Henry became a symbol for Cherokee. Dressed as a Hollywood portrayal of an "Indian Chief," Chief Henry stood for photos for one dollar a shot and put five of his children through college while entertaining visitors who wanted to meet and pose with him.

His rates did go up to five dollars a picture, but it was still well worth it.

Chief Henry became an ambassador of sorts, loving every minute of posing and directing people to the numerous cultural areas of Cherokee. It didn't matter to him or to the visitors that he was dressed in an outfit more suited to a native of the plains than a woodland Cherokee, or that he stood in front of a teepee, which the Cherokee never used. Chief Henry filled a need for people to actually meet an actual Cherokee, and if he got rich on it, more power to him.

In addition to the numerous gift shops and *Unto These Hills*, there is the Museum of the Cherokee Indian, the Oconaluftee Village, Qualla Arts and Crafts, and Oconaluftee Islands Park, a lush green island in the middle of the river that runs through Cherokee. There's plenty to see and do in the town.

Chief Henry passed away on November 19, 2007, after five decades of work. But Cherokee moves on. In 1995, Harrah's opened a casino and resort in Cherokee, changing the economic landscape for the local population drastically. Today Cherokee is more than the kitsch of teepees and souvenirs or photographs with a chief in a headdress. Cherokee is now both a destination and a beginning. It is a place both to stop and rest, and to start your journey into nature.

Oddity

Great retro kitsch, history, and a fancy place to stay. What more could you want?

Difficulty

Make sure you just don't stop at one part of Cherokee. The area has a lot to offer, including lots of great classic motel signs from the '50s and '60s.

Chief Henry's sign is stored in Cullowhee at Western Carolina University's Mountain Heritage Center.

Road to Nowhere

Bryson City 35.45895° -83.53785°

It goes by Lakeview Drive, Lakeshore Trail, North Shore Road, or Fontana Road, but it is best known as the Road To Nowhere.

In the 1940s, the federal government and the Tennessee Valley Authority built the Fontana Dam, in order to bring power to the energy starved Tennessee Valley during World War II. In order to do that, over 1300 families had to be relocated. The local road and several towns were inundated, leaving the displaced families with no access to their ancestral cemeteries on the other side of the newly formed lake. As part of the deal of taking the houses of the locals, the government was supposed to build a road across the north side of Lake Fontana, in order to pave a way into the old graveyards.

The road was supposed to stretch 30 miles, from Bryson City to Fontana. It stopped at 6.

Building of the road was stopped due to an environmental issue 6 miles in right after a tunnel. The environmental issue was resolved, but the work never continued. The original highway can be seen when the water levels are low. A hike to 35.43581° -83.48801° will lead to a n old bridge that is submerged in Spring, but visible when the water is low.

The current road stretches through the Great Smoky Mountains National Park, creating a slow and sedate drive. Then, it just ends before a tunnel. Now, Swain County has a beautiful 6 mile, or 12 mile, since you have to turn around at the end, road to nowhere.

Oddity ★

The views along the road are spectacular in the fall. Too bad that wasn't the original intention.

Difficulty ★★

Everett Street turns into Fontana Road in Bryson City. It's the only road west of Bryson City that goes nowhere. You'll know you are on the right road when you see the "Broken Promise" sign. There is a parking area just before the tunnel, and the road is blocked right after that with metal posts. Don't speed through here! You are in the mountains and it's twisty; be careful.

The cause of all this, the Fontana Dam, is the tallest dam in the eastern US, and was the fourth largest in the world when built. Fontana Village, a nearby resort, was originally Welch Cove, the home of the dam's workers during the building phase. Staying there today requires a lot less work than in 1943.

World's Largest Ten Commandments

Murphy 35.12084° -84.25052°

Fields of the Wood Bible Park is best known for its gigantic Ten Commandments. The hillside replica of God's law given to Moses is 300 feet wide, with huge 5 feet high concrete letters. The Commandments are framed to make a giant set of tablets, with stairs running through the middle to what they claim to be the world's largest New Testament, with passages from the book of Matthew. The New Testament also serves as an observation platform to look down on the (now upside down) Commandments. If climbing to the top of the commandments is too much of a hike, there is an access road that leads to the top.

But there is so much more to see at Fields of the Wood. That's why driving the access road might be a good idea. There's going to be a lot of walking at this place. There is the All Nations Cross, with flags from different nations representing the nations that have received the Word of God. Across from the Ten Commandments is a baptismal pool. The Bethlehem star sits atop a metal tower at the entrance. The Hidden Treasures gift shop sells Christian gifts, books, and knickknacks. Tour the tomb of Jesus, including a stone you, or your kids, can roll back. Prayer Mountain is only 320 steps to the top (there is a longer access road for this as well.)

Fields of the Wood certainly has a very spiritual presence. Whether you go for the religious experience, or just to experience another world's record, it certainly is a site to see.

Oddity ★★

Tick off another world record on your log book, and say a prayer or two.

Difficulty ★

The 18 mile drive from Murphy is a beautiful trip, and you may feel a little lighter of heart on the drive back.

Did You See That? 279

Afterword

I can't believe it has been over ten years since I first started work on this book. Looking back on all the time I spent creating Did You See That? really brings back the memories. Sometimes it feels just like yesterday, then I look at all the pictures and see just how much things have changed over the last decade. I went to a lot of these places with my wife and daughter, who was an infant at the time. Some were just day trips, while others were long drives far away, added on to a quick vacation weekend. And then there were those wild trips I did alone in the convertible, wild all day runs to get photographs of several places at one time. Researching this book and going to all these places was fun, adventurous, exciting, and fulfilling for me. We would turn a day trip into a longer trip when I would say, "I just need to take this little side road...", thinking it would only add a few minutes but in reality adding almost an hour.

Now, ten years later, I just can't do those things anymore. No, it's not because I'm older, worn down from years of exploring, though I did sell the convertible. It's just that now I enjoy being settled with my family. My daughter is no longer an infant, but a grown up young person, smart and inquisitive. We still love to travel, but we like to get there, wherever "there" might be. I have done this four times now, with four books in the Did You See That? series. I've been "there" and got the pictures to prove it.

But that doesn't mean we are going to stop. Now it is less likely that we will take that hour long side trip on an already five hour journey. But we will go out whenever we can, just to go looking for something. While I'm out looking for shipwrecks, there's my family, looking for shells. When I'm photographing mountains, my daughter is soaking her toes in a stream by a waterfall. In my original afterword, I said that we should be thankful for the people that put up with our silly desires to go out and look for weird stuff off the beaten path. Now, ten years on, I also know the value of that adventure we all have together. Always, always get out.

Take your friends and family. You'll never regret a great trip together. Let everyone make the discovery they want, find what they like. Just know that today is a good day to go exploring. Or tomorrow. The rewards of being out there, being with others, or meeting others if you are on your own, are so great. They are the stories you will tell when you get back. They will be in the books you write. They will sparkle in your eyes when other people ask what have you been up to.

There is no rough gem chiseled out of a mountain cliff, no salt polished pirate gold found on the beach that will be as valuable. Ten years ago, it was just an idea that this might be fun. Now it's a promise that you'll have memories and stories and shared experiences. Get out and go, you roadrunners.

Joe Sledge Feb 2021

Acknowledgements

Big thanks go out to the following: Eddie Westbrook from N.C.H.A.G.S., Richard Starbuck of the Wachovia Historical Society, Will Royston from the North Carolina Ghost Guide, Steve Nichols at Discover the Smokies, David Payne from Cooper-Payne Tree Farms, Hannah Raines at the Wilkes Chamber of Commerce, Mark File at Romantic Asheville, Michael Edwards, president of the Hermit Society, Teresa Dowd of the West Carolina Internet Café, Anne White and Lee McMaster from the Elizabethan Gardens, Karen Kornegay, marketing manager for the Morehead Planetarium, Stephen Chalker from TCOM, Dawn Williams from Preservation North Carolina, Donna Bailey-Taylor from the Smithfield/Johnson County Visitors Bureau, Kristy Hill-Hinnant from Hills of Snow, Maureen Daly, Cultural Arts Administrator of the Rocky Mount Arts Center, John Krahnert of the (Southern Pines) Pilot, Janet Leith, manager at the Bordeaux Center in Fayetteville, Leslie Fann of the Museum of Life and Science in Durham, Doug Stover at the Fort Raleigh National Historic Site, Linda Ward of the Town of Lake Lure, Roman Blahoski from Archer Daniels Midland, Eryn Moller, Planner for the Town of Wrightsville Beach.

Photo credits

All photos by Joe Sledge, except
 British Cemetery – Joyce Sledge
Live Oaks of Ocracoke - John Sledge III
World's Largest Hammock – Ann Carden
TCOM Blimp hangar fire, Pink Floyd blimp – Courtesy of Stephen Chalker at elizcity.com
TCOM hangar (current day) – Bill Sledge
CSS Neuse and CSS Neuse II – John B. Sledge, Jr.
Mysterious Hoof Prints at Bath – Will Royston, North Carolina Ghost Guide
Brady Jefcoat Museum (2) – Bill Sledge
First Hardee's (black & white) – Courtesy of N.C. State Archives, State

Historic Preservation Office
Soul City - released into public domain by Tijuana Brass
Morehead Sundial –Ken Bloch Jr.
Gimghoul Castle – Michelle Sledge
Land of Oz (2) – Jim Cary
PARI Dish – David Ploenzke
Bear Shadow – Ed Shearin, Brevard, NC
World's Largest Ten Commandments/Fields of the Wood – courtesy of Steve & Carolyn Nichols, Fields of the Wood

All photographs used by permission. No photographs may be copied, duplicated or used in any way without written permission from the owner of the photograph.

A great big thank you goes out to those people who gave permission for their photographs to be used in this book. You helped complete my book. Some took pictures I couldn't get, and some took pictures that were just way better than what I could do. A great deal of love and respect goes out to my fellow photographers. May you all be blessed with adventures and stories to tell.

About The Author

Joe Sledge is a North Carolina native and graduate of the University of North Carolina at Chapel Hill where he developed a love for exploring. A native of the Outer Banks, Joe traveled across the country and lived in Monterey, CA, where he married his wife, Michelle. After ten years on the west coast, they moved back to North Carolina and currently live in the Piedmont with their daughter. Joe worked for nine years as a special education teacher before writing this book. He and his family find any excuse to go to the beach or travel throughout the state. He is the author of six books, including the four book series of Did You See That?